Don Carrazza

MY STORY

Living in Opportunity

First published by Busybird Publishing 2021

Copyright © 2021 Donata Carrazza

ISBN:
Paperback: 978-1-922691-18-7
Hardcover: 978-1-922691-19-4

This work is copyright. No part of this publication may be reproduced, stored in a retrieval system or transmitted in any form or by any means, electronic, mechanical, photocopying, recording or otherwise, without the prior written permission of Bette Leone.

The information in this book is based on the author's experiences and opinions. The author and publisher disclaim responsibility for any adverse consequences, which may result from use of the information contained herein. Permission to use any external content has been sought by the author. Any breaches will be rectified in further editions of the book.

Cover design: Busybird Publishing

Layout and typesetting: Busybird Publishing

Busybird Publishing
2/118 Para Road
Montmorency, Victoria
Australia 3094
www.busybird.com.au

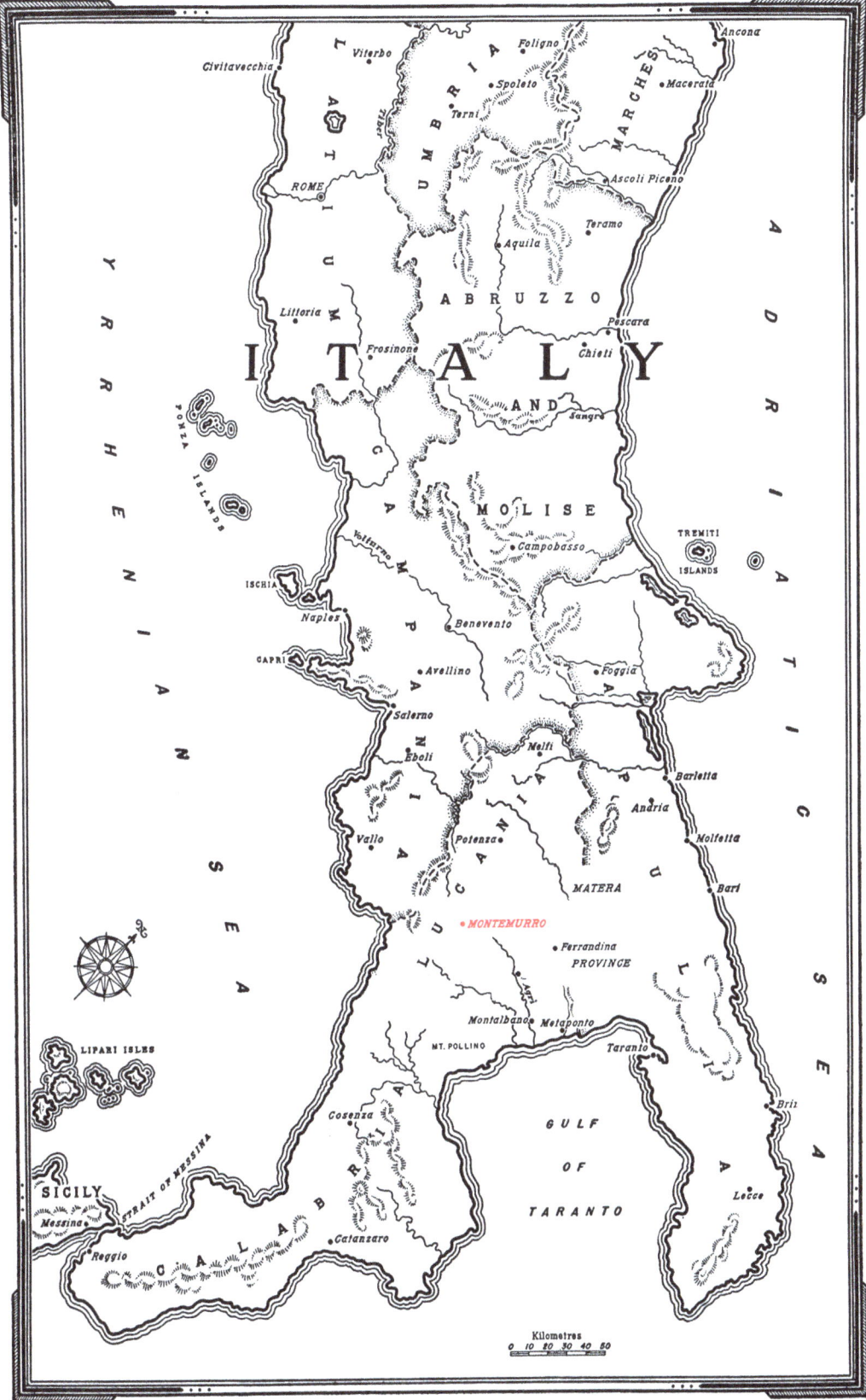

Contents

My Heritage   1
Growing up in Italy   9
Australia Beckons   25
Early Days in Australia   31
Bellboy   35
The Mary Elizabeth   43
Miss Riverland   57
Dominic's   65
Don the Manufacturer   71
Popular Alm   77
Riverside Village and Piccola Italia   81
The Bellboy Comes Home   85
Mildura's Unrealised Jewel   107
Creating Jobs (Real Jobs)   113
Serving the Community   121
Aspirations for a Tourist Town   131
La Famiglia   135
More Family   151
Far from Finished   159

Tributes   163
Acknowledgements   179

My Heritage

Mildura is a huge part of my life. It has been home since I was a young man, a boy really, but this story starts in another place that is dear to my heart and that's Montemurro. Montemurro is a village in the Italian province of Potenza, in the region of Basilicata, also called Lucania, in southern Italy, close to the instep of the boot if you're looking at a map of the peninsula.

Histories of Montemurro record it as being known for olives, chestnuts, the leather industry and, since the 1960s, oil wells. For me, it is where family origins lie.

Both sets of grandparents were born and lived there, though my father's family had originally come from Spain. Apparently, our name was Carranza, a Spanish name, but when the family first got to Italy, the officials replaced the n with a z, so it became Carrazza. It's no wonder there are so few other Carrazzas in Italy. The Spaniards were amongst the many who played a role in southern Italy over the centuries.

Our family were all farmers, as was just about everyone in Montemurro. My grandfather on Dad's side, Domenico (4/8/1882–1/11/1976), was an adventurous type. I think he was born like that. In 1895, at just thirteen years old, he took off to Brazil following his older brother, Giambattista, who was then twenty-one and living in São Paulo. Domenico was fortunate on the ship there, as one of the other passengers was an older *montemurrese* who kept an eye on him on board. Unfortunately, there was no one keeping an eye on the ship's captain who, by some accounts, got involved with a few female passengers and neglected his steering duties—at least his official steering duties. As a result, the ship hit a reef off the coast of Africa and had to dock for repairs, which added 48 days to the journey.

In the meantime, Giambattista had turned up at the destination port in Brazil on the expected due date, only to find no ship and no brother. He didn't know whether Domenico had drowned, was lost, had missed boarding, or if something had happened to the ship. He went back every day for a week before giving up.

Several weeks later, Domenico finally made it to his destination, though, of course, there was no one to meet him. Fortunately, the man who helped my grandfather on the ship insisted that Domenico go with him to his relative's house. Over the next few days, the man managed to track Giambattista down, but Domenico chose not to go and live with Giambattista. The problem was, his brother was shacked up with an indigenous Brazilian woman, something of a no-no as far as Domenico was concerned. So, Domenico preferred to take his chances on the streets of São Paulo. Remember: while Giambattista had been in Brazil for some time, and had obviously had his values influenced by the South American way of life, Montemurro was far from a permissive society. It was Catholic territory, and Domenico had been steeped in those conservative traditions.

Domenico spent a couple of years doing odd jobs and living by his wits, then, when he was fifteen, opportunity knocked. Being good looking, street smart and wise, he had caught the attention of an Italian businessman in São Paulo. This man had been awarded the contract to build a railroad from São Paulo to Rio De Janeiro. He must have seen potential in my grandfather, and he offered Domenico the contract to supply bread to all his workers. He even offered to set Domenico up with an oven and all the other equipment he would need. My grandfather told this man that he had never baked bread in his life, but the Italian insisted. So, while the job was in the planning stage, Domenico practiced making bread. He later told me, 'One day I'd burn it, the next it was hard as rock. I threw so much away but eventually I perfected it.'

Once the project was up and running, things went smoothly at first. The workers started at the São Paulo end, so Domenico didn't have far to travel. As the railroad was getting deeper into the jungle, he realised he needed some transport to carry his bread. So, he bought himself two mules. Once a week he would load the mules up with bread, lead them into the jungle, deliver his bread, collect his cash, lead the mules back, and start baking again.

Domenico had a good thing going but he had his eye on even more riches. His bakery was close to a church that was attended on Sundays by most of the Italian–Brazilians in the area. He didn't bake bread for the railway workers on Sundays, so his ovens were idle—but not for long. He decided to try making and selling sweet rolls to the Sunday worshippers. He would bake normal rolls, brush a sweet substance over the top, and bake them. They sold like, well, hot cakes, and every Sunday the worshippers would line up outside his bakery before and after service. Money was rolling in, so much so that someone warned Domenico to be careful. 'One day in the jungle, they're going to take your mules, strip you naked, and if they don't kill you, they'll take all your money and leave you on the railway.'

And that's exactly what happened. A group of men took his mules and stole his cash. They didn't kill him, but they scared him so much that when he returned to São Paulo he went straight to the contractor and told him there'd be no more bread deliveries.

On his twenty-first birthday, Domenico returned to Italy with the intention of finding a wife. He met my grandmother, Donata Zaccaria (19/6/1896–1/5/1967), but then took off to make his fortune overseas—this time to America, where his other two brothers, Giovanni and Nicola, lived. He started a shoeshining business near Wall Street, and before long had ten or fifteen African-Americans polishing shoes for him. He made a good quid out of that. He'd promised my grandmother that when he turned 25 he would return to Italy and marry her and he remained true to his word. They had five children, my father being one of them, and he made several trips back and forward to America. At the age of 46, he bought an olive grove in Montemurro and basically retired. They lived fairly comfortably, always providing for the family. Food was never missing from the table, at a time and a place where many households could not make the same claim.

Domenico Carrazza and Donata Zaccaria

My grandfather on Mum's side was also called Domenico (that's two so far): Domenico Antonio Liuzzi. My brother, Antonio, was named after him. He had a very different personality to the other Domenico. He was a dominant figure and became wealthy. He farmed and traded and employed a lot of people. He did very little physical work himself. His wife was Antonia, who was a beautiful woman with a very good heart. They had eight children, and my mother, Leonarda, was the third oldest. In order, they were: Leonora, Carmela, Leonarda, Giacinto, Rocco, Felice, Antonietta, and Donato.

Of course, coming from such a small village, both sets of grandparents knew each other.

My father, Giuseppe, was born in 1914; my mother, Leonarda Liuzzi was born in 1919. They were married in 1937. Leonarda's father gave his daughter a forty thousand lire inheritance payment on her marriage and told her to put it straight into the post office holding account (they didn't have any banks in the village in those days).

Before World War II, Dad started an espresso bar called *Il Circolo Dopo Lavoro* (The After Work Club). He bought one of the first espresso machines in Montemurro, an *Aquila* (Italian for eagle). After a while, he wanted to renovate the bar and asked my mother if she would draw some of the money from the post office account. My mother was very innocent about financial matters, so she went and asked her father's advice. He told her not to give Giuseppe anything because, 'When he gets the money, he goes and then you lose him forever.'

So, the funds stayed where they were, until 1963, when a few of us went back to Italy for a trip. We decided to withdraw the money but the local post office had transferred it to a larger post office in another district. Eight of us (my brother, Mum, dad, an aunty, uncle, two cousins and I) trudged to the other district, took the money out and spent it on lunch in a restaurant in Potenza. We had a fantastic time, laughed a lot, but the funds had depreciated so much that there was hardly enough to pay the bill. At the time it was banked it was a fortune. Had it been invested wisely, perhaps we would never have come to Australia!

My father had the espresso bar until 1939 when World War II broke out. He was conscripted into the army, and six months after he had left home, I was born. The coffee machine, a beautiful piece of ornate machinery was kept safe wrapped in blankets in a trunk at my grandmother Donata's home. I wonder if this is where my later fascination with opening a café came from.

*

Montemurro is not what it used to be. It's changed for the worse, and the main reason is the burgeoning oil industry that emerged after the discovery of oil and gas in the region. The extraction of oil has resulted in some areas being consumed by fumes, while the lush, fertile soil on the flat side, where vegetables and fruit were grown, is no more. Nothing grows there. The waters have been polluted. And a recent medical study showed that while seven people died from cancer in the village from 1999 to 2009, in the last decade that number soared to more than 400.

I have a friend who's a journalist and he's fighting to get the place back on track, but it's probably too late. There's nothing anyone can do about it. There are now more people from Montemurro living in Melbourne than in Montemurro itself. As the old people die, there are few young ones replacing them.

It still feels like home to me, even though most friends and family are now long gone. When I'm there, I spend a lot of time at the cemetery, walking around the graves, remembering the people who shared the village life with me.

Montemurro has a long, rich past, but I fear its future. Most of its residents have migrated all over the world. With the population now only just about 1000 (from 8000 in the early 1900s), with few economic prospects and relative isolation from the rest of Italy, it is unlikely a revival will happen. Montemurro has survived a massive landslide, incidentally, but the effects of globalisation might truly wipe the town off the map.

Growing up in Italy

I was born at 11 pm on 27th December 1939. However, I am registered as having been born on the 1st January 1940. Back then, babies were born at home so it could take time for them to be officially registered. While most babies had their real birthdate put on the official forms, there was a reason my mother chose not to.

Baby Domenico, 8 months, 1940

With my father conscripted to fight, war was uppermost in everyone's mind. Men were conscripted from a certain age. With no idea when this war would end, or whether another would start, my mother ensured that I had an extra year's grace in the event of conscription. Now, that's what I call thinking ahead.

Pagliaccio

With Dad away, my early years were spent living at his parents' house with my mother. My grandmother, Donata, was incredible in the kitchen. Whenever she cooked, the aroma would waft outside, fill the air and drive people crazy. People passing would say, 'That's Donata Carrazza cooking.' Everything she cooked had flavour, from *ragù* to *involtini*.

Even her most simple omelettes were special. And, she spoiled me rotten. We lived upstairs and my grandparents lived downstairs. I had never met dad at this point, and grew up learning to read with my grandparents. Being the only grandson then, and being named after her husband, in my grandmother's eyes, I was the kingpin. She grew all her own fruit and vegetables, and every first fruit picked off a tree, I'd be the one to taste it. She wouldn't give it to anyone but her grandson. It's hardly surprising that I've got wonderful memories of my grandmother, and today, habitually place myself at the head of the table!

When I started at school, some of the young kids, from poorer backgrounds, would follow me home and I'd grab something off the bench in the kitchen and give it to them. One of my closest school friends was extremely destitute. He would follow me home, often without me knowing, stand at the door and cough a few times, just loud enough for me to hear. I can still recall those big eyes opening up twice the normal size when I gave him food. The poor boy was literally starving.

Donata died in 1967 but Domenico lived to be 95. When my brother, Antonio, got married in Mildura on 14 October 1972 my grandfather flew out for the wedding. He even made it onto the front page of *The Sun*, because he was the then oldest visitor to Australia at 76 years old. You might wonder how the paper got to know about this. I have to put my hand up to being responsible. I knew someone who worked at the newspaper and briefed him in advance that Domenico was coming out.

Bisleri advertising with nonno Domenico

Once here, Domenico decided not to return to Italy. His three sons were in Australia, my wife adored him—he was spoiled—and he felt he didn't have anybody to whom to go back. He even became the face of a liqueur brand, which had been another one of my ideas. I spoke to Carlo Valmorbida, head of the Valmorbida family company, which imported *Bisleri Ferro-China* from Italy. I proposed they use Domenico as part of their marketing strategy, to suggest their product promoted a long, healthy life. Carlo took me up on the offer and for the next three years, Domenico's image was used to promote *Bisleri*, and the Carrazza family received regular and large supplies of *Ferro-China*.

While Nonna Donata was generous with food and affection, I remember my other grandmother, Antonia, as being generous with money. Every time it was a saint's day (a special day in Italy, where it is almost treated as everyone's birthday), she would give me 5 or 10 lire. Of course, they had the money to be able to do that.

I spent many summers on Antonia's and Domenico Antonio's farm. Harvesting time was particularly exciting for me as I was allowed to follow the bullocks and stand on the huge stone that crushed the wheat. All the family lent a hand at harvest time, so I got to pass time with my cousins. Sometimes we'd walk the 3-4 kilometres to the top of the hill to get the whole view of the village, the lake and the mountains. It was spectacular.

Not having my father around, I had a bit of a constrained early childhood, as Mum was very protective. Because we didn't have a backyard in which to play, the street became the playground for me and my mates. Mum would give strict instructions on when to be home. Five minutes late, I was in trouble, and as a result, I learnt quickly to be home on time, and that discipline of timing has stuck with me throughout my life. I am very punctual, whether to a business meeting or to meet family or friends. One of my grandchildren might say even a little too early!

Among the games we played in the street, one was called *monete rosse*. It involved tossing coins against a wall and whoever got their coin closest won all the other coins that had been tossed. I was good at it. Whenever there was a dispute as to which coin was closest, we would use our hands to measure the distance. I was usually called upon to do the measuring because my hands are large.

Years later, I met a poet, Leonardo Sinisgalli, who had grown up in Montemurro, moved to Rome, but returned regularly and spent many summers back in our village. As we spoke, he recalled watching boys tossing coins (undoubtedly, I had been one of them), and while I reminisced about the game, and filled him in on how it worked, I noticed he was taking notes. Years later, I was alerted to a book by Leonardo that contained a poem titled, *Monete Rosse* (see pages 16 & 17 for original and translation).

Even though I lived in this small Italian village, we were not isolated from the war. I recall a nearby village being bombarded, and hiding with some of my family under a big rock, in case we were next. Who knows how much protection the rock really offered, and there were probably limbs sticking out from the sides anyway. Nonna Antonia was the only one who wasn't too concerned. She would remain in the kitchen making pasta as planes flew overhead and bombs were dropped nearby. She would tell us, 'They're not going to bombard us here because there's nothing to bomb.' She was right; the planes always flew straight past and dropped the bombs elsewhere.

Dad came home when the war ended. Our family heard nothing from him for the first few years of the war—they didn't even know whether he was dead or alive. When another local man came home from the war, ill, in 1944, he told my mother and grandparents that Dad had gone to Albania. That turned out to be true. At the first opportunity, he had fled the front, because of his abhorrence of Mussolini and the Nazis, and gone to Albania where he was befriended by a farming family, who he lived with until the war was over.

This Albanian family not only saved him from possible death, either in war or as a deserter, but they treated him like a son. Unfortunately, after the war, he never got to see them again. Albania was closed to the world until 1987, and there was no way to get in during the four decades before then. When the Albanian government started to loosen restrictions, I bought a ticket for him to travel back to Albania. He was so excited. He was due to fly out in July 1988, but he had a heart attack and died a month beforehand, on 13th June. One of the saddest things I have in my heart is that I never got any details from my father about that family. He never gave us their name, the name of their village, or even which part of Albania they were in. I would love to go back and thank them. I believe part of his reserve was related to the shame he felt about escaping the frontline, despite his conscientious objections. He knew many of the men he had fought with had been captured and sentenced, and that he had saved himself, and lived in relative safety during the war. All this is supposition, of course, because he never spoke about it.

Monete Rosse

I fanciulli battono le monete rosse

contro il muro. (Cadono distanti

per terra con dolce rumore.) Gridano

a squarciagola in un fuoco di guerra.

Si scambiano motti superbi

e dolcissime ingiurie. La sera

incendia le fronti, infuria i capelli.

Sulle selci calda è come sangue.

Il piazzale torna calmo.

Una moneta battuta si posa

vicino all'altra alla misura di un palmo.

Il fanciullo preme sulla terra

la sua mano vittoriosa.

Copper Pennies

The children fling copper pennies

against the wall. (They fall distantly

on the ground with a sweet sound). They yell

lustily in a fire of war.

They exchange proud mottos

and sweet insults. The night

burns their brows, rages their hair.

It's like blood on the hot pavement.

The piazza is calm again.

A thrown coin lands

near another, the distance of a palm.

The child presses his winning hand

into the ground.

(Translation Donata Carrazza)

(While researching old family documents and photos for this book I came across a note written by my father that detailed every location he was in during the war. Finally, I now know that he was based in a city called Gjirokaster in Albania).

Dad's return home was the first time I met him. We had no idea he was coming home until he was almost here. He'd caught the train from Brindisi to Potenza, then took the bus from Potenza to Montemurro. The bus stopped about four kilometres from our village, so he walked the rest of the way. And word got to us while he was on that final walk.

My grandmother was full of joy. She grabbed me by the hand and dragged me outside to meet this man who I had been told was my father, but I think I was probably more concerned about how his presence may disrupt the status quo. I was also very shy, and when he arrived, I hid behind my grandmother's frock. I guess I just hadn't known what to expect. I'd seen photos but here he was in the flesh. He was a six-footer, well groomed, in his army uniform and carrying a gun. From behind my grandmother, he looked very powerful to me.

Those years of absence certainly affected our relationship. At first, he was a stranger and I felt little affection towards him, which (in hindsight) was hardly a surprise. After all, there I was, six years old and all of a sudden this bloke comes into my life and takes over *my* territory. Before he returned, I would sleep in Mum's bed. The fact that Mum and dad had two more sons in the three years after dad's return, shows that I was immediately banished to my own bed. My brother, Antonio, was born in 1946, and Rocco in 1948. Unfortunately, Rocco died at just eighteen months of age from dysentery.

Many times throughout life, I watched fathers with their young sons, and wondered what could have been. Would I have grown up a different person if he had not exited my life virtually before it had begun, and then missed those formative years? Would my life have taken a different path? Of course, late in his life, dad and I became very close and developed a great deal of respect for each other. On 13 June 1988, he suffered that massive heart attack on the family property, whilst he was loading his sheep to go to the local market. A farm worker who saw it happen raced to our house and alerted me. I jumped in the car, drove to the shed and tried to resuscitate him, but I was too late. There was some solace in the knowledge that when he died, he did so knowing he had a good friend in me, not just a son.

I started school around the time dad got home after the war. Although everyone was Catholic, I was taught by teachers, not by nuns. There were nuns around the school, of course, as the school was close to the church, and they used to give us sweets. During the war, whenever there were American soldiers in the village, the nuns would come out and hand them sweets. Of course, we weren't far behind — and we weren't forgotten.

I made a lot of friends quickly at school, some of whom I already knew of course. Back then, you had to make friends. They were your entertainment. It wasn't like today where it seems everyone's best friend is on, or possibly is, their phone. We'd take turns visiting each other's houses and playing. Those days are full of happy memories. I also remember the local council employee having to clear the road for us whenever it snowed, which was a lot in winter.

The classrooms were full, 30–40 kids in each, some with shoes, some without. There was a fair amount of poverty, and some of the kids came to school hungry. Most of the teachers were there for good. Once they arrived at the school, few left. I remember one who, when it was freezing cold would wear a cloak, and he would put the kids under the cloak and walk with them, so they wouldn't get cold walking outside or from room to room.

Dad disappeared out of life again around the time I finished primary school. Making a decent living in post-war Italy was not easy. He did his best and showed an aptitude for trading. He would buy, fatten and then sell sheep, cattle, goats and pigs. But the lack of real opportunities frustrated him. His uncle, Giovanni Sinisgalli (no relation to the poet), had migrated to Australia in 1927, and regularly reported through his letters the opportunities to be had on the other side of the world. He'd started as a fruit picker, and now owned his own farm. Dad and two of his cousins got Giovanni to sponsor them, and in February 1952 they embarked in Naples on the *Cristoforo Colombo*, landing in Melbourne and then going directly to Mildura by train.

Two years later, my father's brother, Francesco, decided to migrate, and my father thought it was a good opportunity for me to travel with my uncle, and join him. The application forms had been completed and my passport obtained. Mum, though, insisted that I stay in Italy. She thought I was too young and should do some more schooling first. She was right: those three years of high school I completed in Italy gave me a solid grounding for later life.

The Italian high school was a boarding school in Lagonegro, fifty-five kilometres away from home. I was lucky to win a scholarship there, after receiving the Diploma of Merit at the end of primary school. That first trip to high school was my first time on a train. An uncle, Donato, Mum's younger brother, was at teachers' college in Lagonegro, and promised to keep an eye on me. Being his nephew gained me a lot of respect, as he was a bit of a local Casanova, you see. He helped me avoid being a victim of a small racket that went on at school. Village mothers would send their young sons parcels and baskets of supplies—*salumi*, cheeses, olives, and other goodies—but the older students would grab them and devour the stuff. Thanks to this relationship with *zio* Donato, though, I was off-limits.

We slept and ate in the college building, twelve to a room, with common showers. Every morning we would march about half a kilometre to the school. There were no football grounds at the school. If you wanted to play football, you had to go to a nearby ground. It was the only one in town, so all the boys would crowd onto it. Football, in fact sport in general, was not encouraged. We were there to learn.

There was some religious training but it wasn't excessive. There was a church attached to the school and one of the clearest memories from those times was being an altar boy, asked to scent the church with incense. Usually the priest would do it, but he asked me, and I felt like a hero waving that burning censer.

I completed three years of boarding school and passed everything with flying colours. Maths was my favourite subject. What I learnt at boarding school was not restricted to academia. I also learnt to be independent and to stand up for myself. My experiences gave me a great start in life, a foundation for the future. They provided me with a certain confidence that proved so useful later. At the time, though, my focus was not on self-improvement but entirely on making my parents proud, particularly my father. I applied myself at school with this goal always at the forefront of mind.

However, schooling there was cut short when I got word that Mum, Antonio and I were moving to Australia, to be with dad.

Australia Beckons

Locals gather in the village square to farewell those travelling to Australia and South America, Montemurro, May 1955

I'm not exactly sure why, but I felt a sense of excitement on hearing we were moving to Australia. Travel was not an everyday occurrence in Montemurro; going to boarding school on the train was the furthest I had ever been in my life, so a ship, an ocean liner, well that was something else altogether. And it was going to take thirty-three days to cross the oceans. A real adventure beckoned. The ship we were booked on was the *Australia*. It was one of three sister ships, the others being the *Neptunia* and the *Oceania*. In 1962, on a trip back to Italy, I got to travel on both of the other 'sisters'; the *Oceania* from Melbourne, and the *Neptunia* on the return trip. These three ships were owned by the Lloyd Triestino shipping company and were known as the Triestino Trio. The *Australia*'s first voyage was from Naples to Melbourne in April/May 1951. We left Napoli on board the *Australia* on the 4th or 5th November 1955.

Mum didn't want to go to Australia at all. While some of my paternal family had migrated to Australia, no one from her family had. She had hoped that Dad would return to us, rather than us go to him in this new land. She remained the only member of her family to migrate to Australia, in fact anywhere, with all her brothers and sisters making a comfortable living in Italy. To make matters worse, her mother passed away just six months after we arrived in Australia; my mother seemed so far away from home then. If she had been in Montemurro at that time, she would have been on my grandmother's rounds, for on the day she died, my grandmother walked around the village, visited all of her children, except Mum of course, and then went home, lay in bed and passed away. She was only 56 years old. She must have had a presentiment that she was not well. Fortunately, Mum's attitude to her move changed gradually after several years in Australia, to the point where she would never have been persuaded to return to live in Italy.

More than a month on a ship provided time for both adventure and imagination. At a stopover in Port Said, an Egyptian city at the northern end of the Suez Canal, I saw my first ever banana. I had seen them in books, but never in my village. They were as exotic a fruit as existed anywhere. When we were in port, young kids sold bunches of them for one or two lire, bugger all really. I bought loads of them, as did a guy my age who I had befriended on the ship, and we sat in a corner of the top deck, munching through those bananas like monkeys. By the time we finished, and the ship had once again set sail, I never wanted to see or eat a banana again and can't remember eating another to this day—except in fritters, with generous scoops of ice-cream.

Aboard the Australia with mother Leonarda, brother Antonio, aunt Antonietta, cousins Donata, Elizabeth (twins), Vicki and fellow Montemurrese, Tommaso Santomartino, (children unknown), 1955

We docked in Port Melbourne on the morning of 8 December 1955. I'd barely been able to sleep the night before, such was my excitement. I had gotten out of bed very early, and packed our bags, and made sure our suitcases were lined up so that we would be first off the ship. There was a sense that something special was about to happen and that's the feeling that I've had about this country from that point onwards—truly. This country held out a promise that has nearly always delivered.

We were met at the pier by my equally excited father. He was a tall, good-looking man, and had beautiful wavy hair. He was wearing what were obviously his good clothes, no doubt to impress my mother who he had not seen for four years. There was something quite magical about seeing him again, a mystique surrounding him, which is not surprising given at that point, I had been away from my father for two-thirds of my life.

From the ship, we went to *zio* Francesco's house at 684 Lygon Street, Carlton, opposite the Carlton cemetery. We only stayed there for three nights but the whole time the place was packed with various family members, some of whom had been on the ship with us, and others from our village who had arrived in the years before us. The chattering barely receded for a moment.

The first thing we kids did when we got to Francesco's was explore the place. While we stayed at that house most of the time, there was not enough room for everyone to sleep there, so we slept at a house belonging to one of my father's friends, just down the road.

Because it was such a rarity to have so many members of the family in the same place, someone booked a session at a photography studio in Brunswick for a family shot. The photographer's name was Torino and he came from a small village called Viggiano, not far from Montemurro.

Reunited in Melbourne

After three days of merriment and mayhem, we left for Mildura at nine at night on 11 December aboard the Melbourne to Mildura train, which was known as the *Vinelander*. It was a slow, ten-hour trip via Ballarat, and we arrived with the sun already well and truly risen at seven the following morning.

Early Days in Australia

We were picked up at Mildura station in a ute—the best Aussie welcome one can get. The ute was owned by cousins who came from Montemurro and had been in Mildura for some years. Mum sat in the front of the ute, while dad, my brother and I sat in the back with the suitcases. He drove us to dad's property near Buronga, just over the bridge from Mildura, on the New South Wales side of the Murray. It was a seven-acre vegetable produce property my father had bought earlier in the year. He was doing well as a grower, with his produce well-accepted across Victoria. He would get it transported to Melbourne where he had agents who would buy or sell it on his behalf.

Being so close to the Murray River was thrilling for my brother and me; not so for my mother. She was terrified because we couldn't swim, none of us could swim, and the moment we would walk towards the river she would yell out, 'Don't go near the water'. I'm pleased to say, none of the family drowned—but that's because nobody ever went for a swim!

The new school year began in February 1956, just after turning sixteen. The campus was St Joseph's College, a Mildura high school, but due to not speaking a word of English, I was switched to Sacred Heart Primary School. We had left Italy whilst I was in year nine going into year ten, but here in Australia I was inserted into the year six class! This was disappointing, because all the things they were doing I had already done four years beforehand. There were no special classes in English, and I was even put alongside another Italian boy, of Calabrian background, Mario Marziano. We couldn't communicate with each other because he spoke in a Calabrian dialect. This changed over time, though, and we remain mates to this day.

After school and on weekends I was kept busy working on the property, and also helping Dad with contract work picking oranges, beans, peas, whatever, on other properties. At least, we were kept busy doing that for about six months, until Mildura and surrounds were hit by a horrendous flood in July 1956. (The flood changed the course of my life, too, but more on that soon.)

The water level of the Murray and the Darling had been rising for several months, due to higher-than-average rainfalls in Western Queensland, followed by heavy rain in Murray catchment areas including the Murrumbidgee and Lachlan Rivers. We had been building a levee bank in preparation, adding more and more soil each day. It cost us a fortune, with trucks arriving every day with more soil. We had glasshouses full of vegetables, and they would all be wiped out if we could not provide enough protection. To no avail. On the night of 7 July 1956, that levee bank broke.

Dad was the first to be alerted. He woke at about four in the morning to the sound of the trickling of water. He wasn't too concerned at first but decided to at least get up and take a look. He realised almost immediately that things were worse than expected; water was already flowing into the house, up to his knees in places. With the house just two hundred or so metres from the river, this was serious.

Dad woke us all up and shouted for us to get out. We had no time to grab anything, not even clothes. We ran out of the house in our pyjamas, and fled to a neighbour's house, one that was not underwater. It was the middle of winter, so we were cold, wet and miserable. Could you imagine? The mother of the house we fled to instructed her sons to give us clothes, and there we stayed while our house, and everything in it, vanished.

It took seven months for the water to subside. When we came back, all the walls had gone; the plaster had dissolved and washed away. During those months away, we lived in a shed on a property in Trentham Cliffs owned by Rod Stevens. Dad had been doing some share-farming there, growing rockmelons and watermelons. The shed was tiny and had been used to store sulphur, probably for the process of drying sultanas. Yes, the whole place stank.

The episode set us back a long way. Mum got very depressed. She had waited ten years to be permanently reunited as a family. Now, after this drama, she faced impermanence and uncertainty yet again. Was there ever going to be peace in her life again? Financially we struggled. I was still going to school but feeling guilty about doing so, and not helping the family get back on its feet.

I dealt with the guilt for some time but eventually enough was enough. I decided that at sixteen years of age, it was time to start working.

Bellboy

I made the decision to leave school and get a job without speaking to my parents about it, as they would have tried to talk me out of it and insist that I stay at school. In the Italian tradition, they wanted their son to grow up and become a doctor. I knew all that, which I is why I didn't consult with them.

One Friday afternoon, on the way home from school, I called in at the Grand Hotel. It was the first time I had stepped inside what was, to me at least, a daunting façade. I didn't beat around the bush, I told them straight out, 'I'm after a job.' I was interviewed by the manager, John Petrie, and obviously did enough to impress him, because he said 'Yes', amongst other things... The problem was, because of my lack of English, I had no idea what job he had given me.

Over the weekend I had to placate my parents, who continued to insist that I should not worry about work and contributing to the family's income at that stage, that school was far more important. But it was just too unnatural to me to leave them with the debts they had incurred because of the floods, such as the hiring of trucks and earthmovers, both in the flood prevention stage, and the aftermath. So, first thing on the Monday morning, I turned up at The Grand, strode up to front reception and declared, 'I'm Domenico Carrazza and I've got a job here.' I didn't know whether I would be given a toilet brush, a broom, a hoe or dish gloves, all I knew was that I was ready to start.

The girl on the front desk obviously knew what was going on because she told me, 'Yes, you've got a job as a bell boy', and she called over the head porter, a Scotsman named Bernie. He took one look at me and spat, 'You can't work looking like this. Where's your black trousers and white shirt?' Apparently, bellboys dressed in black and white, and I had turned up in casual clothes. If John had mentioned the dress code at the interview, I certainly hadn't understood what was required. Bernie demanded I go home to change but an Italian porter, Jimmy Rullo, overheard and came to the rescue. 'Don't worry, Bernie,' he said. 'I'll look after my countryman.'

Jimmy took me to the staff room, grabbed a spare pair of pants and shirt that he had, and dressed me up for the day. I never forgot that act. I'm known today for being organised but that stands in contrast to how I started my career; without the right clothes and not even knowing what my job was.

The bellboy job lasted about two years and I loved it. It instilled a passion for the service industry. I enjoyed the people and the variety of work. My dedication to the job and the way I treated people meant I got more each week in tips than in wages. I earned three pounds a week from the hotel but took home more than double that.

Then, I was promoted to waiter, working in the dining room. For me, this was reward for the time I had spent improving my English language skills. I read and talked and just learnt and learnt. However, my English was far from perfect, as I discovered the first time I worked in the dining room.

I did not have a good handle on all the wines we sold, and a female cosmetic representative who was dining with us ordered a particular bottle of Riesling. I went back to the servery and asked the barman for the wine, but because my English was not the best, I couldn't pronounce it properly and the barman was in no mood to help me out. Rather than take her the wrong wine, I used some initiative and went back to her with the wine list open, apologised for misunderstanding what she ordered and asked her to point to the wine she wanted. As soon as she took her finger away, I replaced it with mine and walked back to the servery marking the spot. I wasn't giving the barman another opportunity to berate me.

Working as a waiter led me to meet many interesting people, not just locals but also businesspeople and dignitaries passing through. Probably the most memorable of these was the Dutch consul-general, or more accurately, his daughter.

She was about my age, and on one particular day, seemed to be following me everywhere. She must have known my shift times because at the end of shift after the dinner service, I noticed her following me to my car. I had a '35 Chevy, and she expressed some interest in going for a ride.

I was proud of that car. I'd bought it for thirty-five pounds from an ex-pilot, Rod Stevens, who lived in Trentham Cliffs and had taken us in after the floods. He knew his mechanics and the car was in great nick, which is one reason I bought it. Another reason was that it was a convertible. I knew girls would love convertibles, and this one did.

I didn't quite know what to do but I took her for a drive down to the river. In the meantime, her parents kept drinking in the dining room with the hotel manager. It was only when they went up to their room that they noticed, for all intents and purposes, she had disappeared.

The alert went out. Word spread throughout the hotel: did anyone know where she might have gone? The police were even alerted. One of the other waiters knew she'd gone with me but kept quiet.

When we got back, I dropped her off in the laneway next to the hotel. The waiter in-the-know saw us, and told me what was going on and to clear out. Which is exactly what I did.

The next morning, I turned up at work on time as if nothing had happened. I was immediately summoned to the manager's office and he proceeded to give me a blast, telling me I had ruined the reputation of The Grand, and that he was going to sack me. I told him the truth: she had followed me; we went for a drive; nothing happened; and I brought her back. But he didn't believe me.

He told me that he'd deal with me later and to get to work. Soon after, I was in one of the lounges cleaning tables, and the young woman walked in, grabbed me, kissed me on the cheek, and said goodbye. Right in front of the manager. I guess he decided maybe it hadn't all been my fault because he kept me on.

Mind you, he had been out to get me for some time—and continued to. He seemed to be jealous. Maybe he thought that one day I was going to take over his role.

There was another occasion, after I had eaten one of my Mum's specialty dishes. It had spinach, garlic, paprika, hot chilli and lots more garlic. Mum loved garlic. I went to work and started talking to the manager. He told me I reeked of garlic and 'not to come to work like this.' He promptly sent me home.

Those were the days of the six o'clock swill, when pubs had to stop serving drinks at six, unless it was with food in a dining room. We knew the regulars of course, and in the section I often worked in, there was a group from the Commercial Bank of Australia who I got to know well. Mr Vance, the manager, his accountant and a couple of tellers, would come every day but with limited time because after balancing the books they wouldn't close the bank doors until 5.30pm. Then they'd run to The Grand like a mob of sheep to water. I would have everything organised for them. I knew Mr Vance would drink four scotches with a jug of iced water, the accountant would drink four seven-ounce glasses, and also what the others drank, so I would have them all lined up. If they'd had to queue to order, they wouldn't have been served because everyone crowded around the bar to get served approaching six p.m.

I gained respect and earned a lot of brownie points treating Mr Vance and his colleagues in this way. It paid off in spades, with Mr Vance being one of the people who really got me started in business.

In 1959, after I had been at the hotel for nearly three years, an opportunity came my way. A café around the corner came up for sale. This was the first of many business opportunities I have taken in my life, or at least considered. During three years of work at The Grand, almost all of the money from that wage had gone into a personal account at the Commonwealth Bank. Now, my intention for working had been to help Mum and Dad but Mum would have none of it; she insisted I put my earnings into my own account. By the time this café came up on the market, I had saved £2332. I asked the real estate agent how much the owner wanted, and he told me five thousand pounds. I told him I only had £2332, but the next Friday afternoon, while I was on a break, I went to the Commonwealth Bank, a skinny little 19-year-old, strode to the front desk and asked to see the manager.

'What for?' the woman of the front desk asked.

'I want to borrow some money.'

'In that case,' she said, 'you want to see the accountant.'

The accountant was a guy called Bruce, who I knew quite well. So, I went into his office and after asking him to keep our conversation confidential, told him, 'I want to buy the little coffee shop called the Mary Elizabeth.' Straight away I took my passbook out and said, 'This is what I've got in the bank.'

'Who's going to guarantee you the rest?' he asked.

I thought about it for a moment, then told him, 'Well, my father's got nothing. He can't guarantee me.'

'You have to find someone. You can't guarantee yourself, you're not 21.' Then he added, 'You've got a problem. Best you walk away and forget about it.'

The same afternoon, Mr Vance and the others from the Commercial Bank came in. He noticed I wasn't my usual self, and when I asked if I could see him in his office on Monday, he said, 'Yes'.

So, there I was the next Monday morning, standing outside before the bank even opened. I told him my story, that I wanted the café, but they wanted five thousand pounds for it.

He asked who the agent was, and I told him, 'Collie and Tierney.'

'Who's handling it? Collie or Tierney?'

'Frank Tierney.'

So he gets on the phone. 'Frank,' I heard him say. 'I believe the Mary Elizabeth is on the market, for £5000 pounds. Can you do a better deal?'

'No, that's what they want,' Frank tells him. 'They won't take a penny less.'

'Well get a contract organised for Don Carrazza and bring it straight over.'

And I'm sitting there not believing what I'm hearing. I was lost for words.

I told Mr Vance I'd get the money, and I rushed around to the Commonwealth Bank, withdrew my £2332, went straight back to the Commercial Bank, and opened an account. Mr Vance not only lent me the balance I needed, but also enough for all the legal costs, plus he gave me £500 working capital. I could not believe it.

Domenico Carrazza was in business for himself.

The Mary Elizabeth

There was a month between signing the contract for the Mary Elizabeth and officially taking it over. For that month I kept working at The Grand and I made sure that there were scotches ready for Mr Vance every night—he got service plus.

In September 1959, the Mary Elizabeth was mine (37 Langtree Avenue). I immediately went about reinventing the place. It had been run as a tea house by an Englishman, Jim Morgan. Jim was very elegant, always dressed in a cream suit.

My reinvention actually started before I even moved into the place. The way it had operated was so old-school English. There was lace cloth on all the tables, and polished tea pots and silver everywhere. Whenever anybody ordered a tea, a waiter would take over tea pots, water pots, cups, the whole shebang. To my eye, it was a time-consuming rigmarole, a hospitality nightmare. So, the first decision that was made about the place was to get rid of the tea and make coffee the focus.

Now please remember, back then, the notion of a cappuccino, let alone *caffè latte*, was alien to Mildura. Even in Melbourne, I believe there were only five espresso machines, the most famous being at Pellegrini's.

I intended to be the first in Mildura so went down to Melbourne and bought a *Gaggia* three-group coffee machine from an importer in Nicholson Street. It cost 200 pounds, an extraordinary amount of money. You could almost buy a house for that then. I took it back to Mildura so it was ready for my first day of trading. Mildura didn't know what had hit it. It felt extra special given my father had, back in Italy, opened an espresso bar.

The combination of the machine and the pure milk created the perfect froth for a cappuccino. The problem was no-one in Mildura had even seen a coffee with froth. They loved my coffee but they found it hard to accept the froth. They used to scoop the froth off the top of the coffee and scrape it onto their saucers or all over the tablecloths.

Introducing Italian coffee to Mildura was just the start of a café revolution. The Mary Elizabeth shut at nine at night. But just up the road were two cinemas whose features didn't end until about eleven. On top of that, there were dances held in local halls twice a week, one on Wednesdays, the other on Saturdays, and hundreds of people went to those dances.

It made sense to me to stay open later and try to capture some of that business. Of course, there was no way I would be able to cope if everyone came in at the same time, so I bribed (rather, persuaded) some people at the cinemas with free raisin bread and cappuccino, to time their last screenings so that one cinema would finish at least 10 minutes after the other. I was also advertising the business on the cinema screens before the movies started.

With the cinema crowd and the dancehall patrons, I had people queuing outside the café almost every night. In eight months the debts had been paid off and the business was turning a good profit. At that time staff costs were about 6% and the cost of the food was 3-4%; today's restaurateurs and café owners don't even dare dream of those figures.

Things were going well but in April 1960, Mr Vance called me into his office and told me, 'Don, you've got to borrow some more money.'

'More money? I don't want any more money. I've paid you back.'

'It's not about the loan,' he said. 'It's about tax. On the fifteenth of April, you will have a tax bill of about two and a half thousand pounds.'

I almost died. What was he talking about?

He explained that when you make a profit you have to pay tax on it. Of course, I know that now. It seems impossible that someone in business wouldn't know that, but I was young, I was naïve in many of the ways of business. I had a bookkeeper but no accountant.

My Vance recommended an accountant to me, and the accountant went over my books and found that, indeed, I was facing a tax liability of more than two thousand pounds. So, Mr Vance lent me the money to pay my tax, and shortly after that called me in for another meeting.

'I know I've backed the right horse,' he told me, 'but you've got to protect your future.'

At that stage, I wasn't thinking about the future. If life kept going the way it was, it seemed my future was assured. The café was open until one. Mildura was now alive into the early hours. The money was rolling in. Life was beautiful. Who cared about the future?

Fortunately, Mr Vance was more level-headed than I was. He advised me to drive around the town and look for a property on which to grow vines or citrus – produce that could be grown and grown tax-free. I did as he instructed and found sixty acres of land about five kilometres from Mildura.

I went back to Mr Vance, told him I'd found a place, and he asked me to show it to him. He was impressed with my choice. When I told him I didn't have the money to buy it, he told me, 'Don't worry, that's what I'm here for.'

He then asked how much the owners wanted for it. I told him eight and a half thousand pounds and he said to tell them I'll take it. Mr Vance wrote them out a cheque for the whole amount – there were no formalities around a deposit, or anything like that.

Despite having bought the café, this was my first proper introduction to the world of business; or at least the first time I had really paid attention to it. I have never forgotten Mr Vance's support. It could be said that I would not have got where I did without the backing of such a big-picture man.

That property became the location for our first home. My daughter, Maria, and her husband Mario and their children, live on that land today.

While the café business was thriving, Dad was also going along well. In the late 1950s, he started selling wine grapes to backyard winemakers in Melbourne. No-one else, to my knowledge, had at that point tapped into this market as a niche worth pursuing; but there they were, all these people, Italians mainly, making their own wine at home. Throughout the 1960s, his business grew and grew. He was selling something like fifteen thousand cases a year to these backyard operators and spending three months a year in Melbourne cultivating this business.

While all this wine business was going on around us, not just with Dad but all over Mildura, I was running a dry café. The coffee was bringing people through, as was the food, but I needed a liquor licence, not only to sell wine but even to allow people to bring their own into the Mary Elizabeth.

In 1965 it was time to get a liquor licence. It was not an easy thing to do. Before applying, I had to work in an environment that had a licence. My experience at The Grand could not count and besides, no-one there was going to help me. So, when I spoke to two of my customers one evening, and found they owned the Ritz restaurant in Melbourne, one of the fanciest restaurants in town (where the Marriot Hotel is now), I asked if I could spend time with them. They agreed, I did my required training, and put in my licence application. There, we would serve over 300 lunches a day, especially to parliamentarians. Melbourne was not like it is now, with thousands of restaurants and venues—not even Florentino existed then. (The few options included The Latin, Society, The Ritz, Mario's in Russell Street (very famous), and Molina's on Bourke St.)

One Sunday evening, three weeks from my official hearing for the licence, a young couple walked into the Mary Elizabeth. The house was almost full but a waitress found a couple of seats for them and led them over. I hadn't seen them, as I was flat out, but they were carrying a bottle of Moyston claret. Apparently, they'd been at The Grand and brought it from there. They asked for some glasses, and of course we didn't have any wine glasses, but the waitress gave them a couple of tumblers.

The moment the couple started to pour their wine into their glasses, two coppers walked in, took some notes and booked me for serving liquor in a non-licensed premise. This was a black mark on my credibility and my licence application was turned down. I knew it was a set up, but at the time I couldn't prove it.

Some thirty years later, however, and this man came up to me at a local football club function. He said, 'I'm getting old. I'm going to die like everybody else, so I want to get this off my chest. Do you remember the day a couple came into your place with a bottle of wine, followed by two policemen?'

Of course I did.

'Well, I was one of the policemen, and you were set up by the manager of The Grand, and the local sergeant. They were in cahoots.'

The revelation came as no surprise to me. I had always suspected that the manager of The Grand at that time, who was also one of the major shareholders, had tried to ruin my business and send me broke out of pettiness.

While there were some in Mildura who were jealous, the same was not true of restaurateurs in Melbourne. Quite the opposite. As someone keen to improve and to keep up with trends, every time a restaurant would open in Melbourne, I would jump in my car and drive down to take a look. Then I'd come back and implement some of the things I'd seen. It might be changing the shapes of the table arrangements, or the design of the menu, or putting on a new dish.

The restaurants I visited and often went back to included Molina's, near Parliament House; Pellegrini's of course; Florentino; and The Walnut Tree in North Melbourne. I was this kid from the country who would ask them all the questions under the sun. But they listened and answered because they could feel my passion. To this day, I have friendships that were formed from those experiences.

A touch of Melbourne came to Mildura because of those connections.

Another thing encouraged through the Mary Elizabeth was not necessarily an understanding but at least a strong appreciation of art. At one point in the early sixties, I had fifteen or twenty Pro Hart paintings on the walls of the café, all for sale. Pro would come and eat at the restaurant when he was in town from Broken Hill, and that's how I got to know him. The sale came about at a time when Pro was broke, and he sent these paintings down to me to try to sell for him. He would have been happy with twenty or thirty bucks for each of them, but nobody wanted them. He hadn't become famous yet.

Next to the Mary Elizabeth was a shop called Opal Down Under. The owner had collected opals at Coober Pedy and the shop attracted tourists and others looking for a touch of Australiana. I thought Pro's paintings might sell better in there, so I gave them to the owner on consignment. This was just before Easter and back then, the Easter weekend was the biggest weekend of the year for Mildura tourism. The owner sold all of Pro's paintings over that weekend.

I rang Pro and told him, 'I have a cheque for you.' Well, he couldn't get down here quick enough. I reckon he flew down rather than drove down. The cheque was for $775 and he was so grateful. It was as if he hadn't seen so much money at one time in his life, which may have been the case then.

We kept in touch over the years, and whenever he had an exhibition in town he would pop into Dominic's, the restaurant and club I set up after the Mary Elizabeth, and we would eat and drink and chat. On display at Dominic's, I had a menu from Da Meo Patacca, a restaurant in Rome. He would always sit next to where this menu was displayed and on one occasion, he told me, 'One day, when I make more money, I'm going to go and eat there.'

A few years later, he turned up out of the blue with a couple of paintings tucked under his arm. 'These are for you,' he said. 'For all the things you've done for me.' Then he told me I had to guess where he had painted them. It turned out he had painted them in Da Meo Patacca, while he was eating there with his wife and his sister. They really captured the feeling of a Roman trattoria from the time of La Dolce Vita. Of course, I still have them proudly hanging on my walls.

Da Meo Patacca, Pro Hart

The Mary Elizabeth was closed in 1972, the year our daughter Maria Elizabeth was born, and Dominic's was opened. I couldn't sit still.

For example, in 1960, the Mildura Italian community financed and built a hall. It is still in existence today as the Club da Vinci. When it was completed, I saw how beautiful and practical it was and put my mind towards how I could help make it work, not just for the Italian community but for everyone in Mildura. I went to the president and the committee who had been appointed to manage the hall and asked if I could lease it for a special dance night once a month.

Once the committee agreed, I sprang into action. I was thinking big. I drove down to Melbourne, walked into the office of the general manager of Channel Nine and told him I wanted to book ten of his best artists for the next year.

He looked at me, remember, I was only twenty-one at that stage, and he said, 'Who's going to be guarantor?'

'No-one,' I told him. 'Just me.'

He wasn't convinced at first, but I talked him around by promising to pay for each artist up-front. He saw my passion, we sat down, signed a contract, and I chose the ten artists I wanted. Those artists were the most popular performers of the day: Dorothy Baker, Toni Lamond, Billy McCormack; performers of that ilk.

Back in Mildura I told everyone in sight what I had planned. Word spread and the town of six or seven thousand people couldn't believe that I was going to bring up these famous TV artists. They were so excited, the women started planning which frocks they were going to wear.

Billy McCormack

Dorothy Baker

Toni Lamond

The first dance sold out almost as soon as the tickets went on sale. It was such a success. The band blew everyone away, and the headline was an Irish comedian and singer, who was fantastic. He really got them all up and dancing; what a night.

The next one was booked out before the act was even announced. It, and the ones that followed were smash hits. The problem was, they were too successful. At the end of the twelve-month lease, the committee decided not to renew it. Their thinking was 'Why should he make all the money; we can do it ourselves.'

Of course, they couldn't, and they didn't, and great opportunity was lost to keep the momentum going within the community. I had built this tremendously exciting event that had the town dancing for joy, but it all ended.

The other main venture alongside running the Mary Elizabeth was a gelato bar. It opened on Eighth Street in 1967. We made all the gelato on site and produced gallons and gallons of granita.

One of the most important features of this venture was that it introduced outdoor dining to Mildura. You'd think that with the Mildura climate, outdoor dining would have been around before then, but it wasn't.

To inaugurate the place we invited the mayor and some councillors, and set them up at a table outside and served them gelato and granita. The mayor was not comfortable about it. He said, 'I don't want to be seen sitting down in the middle of the street, what are people going to say about me?' I think he was more concerned about breaking the law. You see, the council was so reactive they wouldn't give me a permit for outdoor dining. But I set it up anyway and everyone loved it. The council officers weren't game enough to book me. They didn't want to approve it. They didn't want to make it official. But they turned a blind eye.

Next door to the gelato bar was a photography studio, there since 1930 and set up by a northern Italian by the name of Frank Zaetta. Frank was a real character: a photographer, a musician, a novelist, a talented actor and painter. He became another notable mentor in my life who introduced me to the famous 'golden stairs' at the Mildura Mens' Club. Thanks to Frank I was nominated as a member of the Club over 50 years ago; I got to walk up those golden stairs as a legitimate and welcome member of the club.

While I set the gelato bar up, I didn't manage it. That task (along with so many others, over the years) fell to Anna, my beautiful wife. So let me tell you how I met Anna.

Miss Riverland

Anna DeVito, 1957

I have my father and his successful grape selling business to thank for meeting, and eventually marrying, Anna, the love of my life.

As Dad's business grew, mainly as a result of an influx of Europeans into Victoria in the late 1950s and early 1960s, he could not source enough red grapes from around Mildura.

Red wine was far more popular among his home brew wine makers than the white varieties, so he established a supply chain that included growers in Renmark, South Australia, an hour or so over the border from Mildura. Despite running my own businesses, including growing grapes, I managed to find the time to help Dad out whenever he needed. Such was the case over Easter in 1963.

Dad needed sixteen semi-trailer loads of red grapes at this time to fulfil orders and he managed to find most of what he wanted. There was still about one truck load to find. I had run out of grapes to supply Dad, so we asked our contact in Renmark, a Mr Johnson, to find some more. He got back to us with the bad news that none of the growers had any more. My Dad was desperate for this last truck load; he had tried everyone else, and I couldn't believe that we couldn't get more from Renmark, of all places. I drove down there, picked up Mr Johnson and we went from property to property in and around Renmark, including Loxton and Barmera. He was right; no-one had a single spare grape.

I was about to do something I hadn't done before: throw my hands in the air and give up. Then, as I dropped Mr Johnson off, he suggested I drive to Waikerie, about fifty kilometres from Renmark, and see this guy there by the name of Joe De Vito. 'He's Italian,' he told me, 'he has a transport business, he's a farmer, he has all the contacts and he might be able to help you.'

It was worth a try. Just as I was about to drive off, he called out, 'Don, if you don't do any business with the grapes, he's got four daughters.' I had heard of Giosuè (Joe) before and knew a little about him. He was very famous in the Riverland, one of the early Italian pioneers in the area. He had arrived there in 1927, four years after his father set down roots there. One of the things I knew was that one of his daughters had been Miss Waikerie and Miss Riverland.

When I got to the property of Giosuè, I introduced myself and told him what I wanted. Unfortunately for me, Giosuè had started doing exactly what my dad was doing, supplying European migrants with grapes to make their own wine. Only he was doing it in Sydney, not Melbourne. As a result, he didn't have any grapes to sell me. In fact, he wanted more as well.

While we were walking around his property talking, I saw a heap of pumpkins in a shed, and asked if they were for sale. I didn't really have a need for them, but I wanted to start a connection with Giosuè—I have always found that buying someone's products is the best way to do this. At the very least, Dad could sell them, as he basically sold anything.

'Sure, you can have them,' he told me. 'I'll put them on my next truck to Melbourne. We'll weigh them there, and I'll drop in to Mildura some time for the money.'

All the while we were talking, I had one eye out for this good-looking girl I had heard about. To no avail; she was at boarding school at St Dominic's Priory College in Adelaide. While I was disappointed not to see her, I told myself that I would meet her one day.

That day happened to be four months later. One of my other sidelines was as an agent selling Peter Stuyvesant and Rothman cigarettes. These were distributed in Australia by Dalgety, which was based in Adelaide. So, one afternoon, with the Mary Elizabeth quiet, I decided to drive to Adelaide to stock up on cigarettes, and, seeing as I was going there, to stop by first in Waikerie. Tick, tick, tick, the brain was working things out.

I booked into the Waikerie Hotel (the Mary Elizabeth would be fine without me for the night) and, seeing as I was so close, drove to the De Vito's property to pay them a visit. You can imagine my surprise, and some degree of mortification, when I pulled into their driveway to see a line of parked cars. A crowd was there for either a funeral or a party. I hoped it was the latter but decided not to intrude either way.

Too late. I was spotted by Giosuè's oldest son, Cosimo (Cosi), who I had met before, and who recognised me and invited me in. I couldn't turn back now, even if I had wanted to.

It turned out that the event was for Giosuè's wife, who was about to travel back to Italy for the first time in over twenty years, and all the friends and the relatives had come by to wish her well. So I joined them. And that's when I first met Anna, in July 1964.

We connected, much to my delight, and chatted well into the night. We spoke about how many people were in the family, which towns they were in, how long we had been in Australia, all sorts of things. The following morning, at my hotel, I thought about dropping in at the De Vito's, in the hope that they would offer me a cup of coffee before I went on to Adelaide. But then I decided to do something a little different, something that would impress them a lot more than an uninvited drop in, the morning after a party.

I drove straight to Adelaide, loaded my car with cigarettes, and then went shopping. Keen to impress, I bought two Neapolitan coffee percolators (Anna's Mum's family was from Naples) and two coffee cups; and under the pretence of thanking them for their hospitality the night before, presented them to Anna and her mother as gifts. In relating this story to my daughters many years later, Donata called me *furbo* (cunning). It's hard to disagree.

Whether it was my charm, my car or the percolators, something worked, because that was the start of a relationship with Anna. We started to call each other regularly and exchange letters, and within twelve months we were engaged. The engagement lasted two years (with Anna in South Australia and me in Mildura) but we finally tied the knot in Waikerie on 25 June, 1966.

It was the wedding of the year in Waikerie, perhaps of the decade. Anna was a very popular and much-loved young woman in the district. The catering was provided by Mr Panebianco, an Italian man originally from Puglia who moved to Melbourne, where his catering business was based. We chartered a bus to transport all the waiters, chefs and supplies from Melbourne to Waikerie.

Four hundred guests packed the Waikerie Town Hall, and apart from the magnificent food and flowing wine, they enjoyed a band, who we brought from Adelaide, and who shared the stage with an electric illuminated fountain we set up. The whole occasion was a little bitter-sweet because Anna then had to leave Waikerie and her family for Mildura, some 200 kilometres away.

We spent the night of our wedding in a modest Barmera motel, a short distance from Waikerie, and the next day drove to Mildura where we had lunch at the Mary Elizabeth with family and guests from Melbourne. After lunch, we drove to Canberra, then Sydney, where we left our car with friends and flew to Surfers Paradise for a two-week honeymoon.

I fell into a beautiful family with the De Vitos. They embraced me fully and we shared many happy occasions. Even now after Anna has died, I am in touch with Tony and Rita, Anna's siblings, especially Rita, who is in contact regularly.

After our wedding, the plan was to move into the house on the property I bought in 1960. Unfortunately, the house wasn't finished by the time we got married. The property had undergone an enormous amount of work, with an irrigation network of pipes and pumps installed, and trees and vines planted as seedlings and saplings.

I designed the house with Tom McCullough, the director of the Mildura Arts Centre and gallery. He had put Mildura on the art map by holding a sculpture triennial that attracted Australian and international artists. There were few architects in town then, and only a few more draughts-people, so we didn't have what one would consider today to be a proper plan. We didn't even take any paperwork to council to get the project signed off with a permit; that only happened after we had built it. That's the way things worked in those days.

The construction of the house started in 1965, with me overseeing a whole bunch of subbies. We used Mount Gambier stone as this was what Anna's Waikerie home was founded upon and hired skilled German tradesmen. We built a glorious-looking house that does not have a crack in it to this day. I have no accurate idea of how much the house cost to build because I'd just use money from here and there, not really track it, and rarely got (or asked for) receipts.

So immediately after we were married, we lived with my parents for two months until the house was ready. Within a few years of moving in, we had two daughters. Donata was born on 20 August 1968, and Maria on 20 April 1972. Anna and I lived happily in that house for 34 years, and then, when we moved, gave it to Maria and Mario, and it is still within the family today.

Engagement party

Dominic's

what can  offer?

FIRST CLASS ENTERTAINMENT
FINE CUISINE : FRIENDLY SERVICE

The Mary Elizabeth Room
... Here you are welcome to dine in a casual atmosphere, where we can provide you with anything from a sandwich to an excellent 'a la Carte' Dinner.

The Continental Room
... Where you can dine and dance nightly in pleasant surroundings with an extensive Gourmet selection, and dance on our White Marble floor.

The Charcoal Room
... Complete privacy is available for you to entertain your friends and provide your own cooking and service in a pleasant atmosphere. If you prefer, you may occupy the room for the evening, and have our waiters provide table service to your guests.

The Reception Room
... Here we cater for Weddings, Conferences, Mannequin Parades, Regular Cabarets and Dinner Dances with First Class Entertainers - in fact, any function.

The Piano Cocktail Bar
... The night spot.

What can Dominic's offer?

By 1970, our family was well-established in Mildura, and our first daughter had been born, named after my grandmother Donata. Life was good, but I have never been one to sit back and smell the roses. Instead, I sought further challenges. Across the road from the Mary Elizabeth was a building I had my eye on. It had been the Murray Moon dance hall and was then the Volkswagen dealership. The success of the Mary Elizabeth, and the memories of the dances I had put on at the Italian club, were enough to spur me on to buy the building and invest something like a quarter of a million dollars into developing Dominic's, with a function room upstairs and restaurants downstairs.

It took some two years to develop the complex, basically gutting the building and starting afresh. Then we had to install all the equipment for the various spaces. Despite the money and the effort, I never wavered in my belief that it would work.

It was a great success from the start. We ran dinner dances in the restaurant six nights a week, unheard of in a country town. The main restaurant had capacity for around eighty people, and it was almost full every one of those six nights of the week.

We had a house band, Jade, that comprised guitar, bass and drums. They would set up in a corner, just in front of a small dance floor – marble mind you – and the patrons would eat, drink, and, when there was room for them, dance. It's got to be said, out of those three activities, it was drinking that was usually priority number one. They drank 'til the cows came home. There were no booze buses or .05 back then.

Upstairs we catered for all sorts of functions: small conferences, weddings, private parties, anything that would fit. Wine tastings became popular as well. I hosted the Wine and Food Society of Mildura and the National Wine Institute Conference; we had tastings with more than 2500 glasses poured–Anna polishing most of them. Anna worked so hard in those days and gave the business so much of herself as did my parents, my brother Tony and his wife, Cathy.

One function, in particular, still springs to mind. It was in the mid-seventies and an Italian wedding was booked for three hundred people. We prepared 150 roast chickens the day before, and that evening, both sets of parents of the couple turned up to see me. There was a fairly lengthy silence before the father of the groom finally spoke, and said, 'My son has disappeared. There will be no wedding tomorrow.' It turned out that the groom had fled to Queensland, leaving a note to say he would never marry the woman who had been chosen by both sets of parents to be his wife. I was more concerned about the 150 roast chickens, but I was most imaginative with the specials board the following week: there was every possible chicken dish we could concoct.

In the back of the section downstairs, there was the Charcoal Room, a private space where small groups could cook their own steaks on a charcoal barbeque. There was also a pizza oven and we sold pizzas in the restaurant and as takeaway. The place buzzed like no other in Mildura. Dominic's employed about 35 people.

For six years, Dominic's was the most visible and successful of the businesses, and a major part of my life. However, by 1978, I was starting to feel a little weary. It was taking its toll, not only on me but also on Anna who was the backbone of the place. I had worked for myself for close to twenty years, so when I received an offer to sell the business, the timing felt right. I kept the building though, and only sold it in the 1990s.

As soon as Dominic's was sold, I took Anna, Donata and Maria for a six-month holiday in Italy. It was a welcome relief for all of us: the business success had caused a fair bit of jealousy in town, and rumours started spreading, including that I was involved in growing and selling marijuana. The girls even experienced some bullying at school over these rumours. Unfortunately, we had to return home earlier than expected after Anna's father was diagnosed with cancer.

Don the Manufacturer

Mildura, and other towns along the Murray, have long been renowned for their citrus fruits, particularly oranges. Despite this, in the mid-1970s, there was only one cooperative orange processing plant in Mildura, the Mildura Co-Op. They survived because they had no competition, so there was an opportunity.

I decided to set up a local cooperative, or rather something similar to a cooperative but with the legal structure of a unit trust, in 1978. It was called Murrayland Fruit Juices. It started with a selection of sixty of the best growers in the district; reliable growers, quality growers, growers who knew how to grow the best oranges. They each contributed $7000 to fund the set-up, and their product provided a secure supply base. I was managing director with a 30% share of the business.

As we were starting up, our board sought a meeting with that of the Mildura Co-Op, just so we could give them the heads-up and assure them there were no hard feelings. Indeed, many of our growers, including myself, had been members of their cooperative. The members of the Mildura Co-Op board were not too concerned; they didn't consider us a threat. In fact, their general manager told us we wouldn't last twelve months. I left that meeting thinking, 'We'll show you.' Show them we did. Within two years we had taken 60% of their business. Much of that was to do with my acknowledgement that I did not know everything about the industry, or even about manufacturing. In fact, I said to the growers, 'I've been in the food industry all my life, hospitality, it's different to manufacturing. This is a new era, a new concept, a new business for me. I don't want to go into it with my eyes closed. We want to know exactly what's involved and what we can do to be better than our opposition.'

I asked for, and received, a six-week overseas trip to check out best practice in the orange manufacturing business. Given their dominance of the global industry, travel involved visiting Israel, Italy, Brazil and the US, particularly Florida and California.

In Israel I saw a machine that was able to capture orange essence from the evaporation of water from the juice (it took ten thousand litres of juice to capture one litre of essence). From there, to Sicily, where I studied the quality of the oranges.

Next stop was Brazil, the largest citrus producer in the world. That was a mind-boggling experience. There were two plants, each of which manufactured product from two million tonnes of oranges each year. There were always eight trucks lined up transporting product in or out; I think there were 250 trucks in total, travelling between growers, and the manufacturers and their customers. But the most amazing thing I learnt was how they extracted oil from the skins of the oranges. It was a by-product common in toothpaste. As if that wasn't fantastic enough, I noticed sacks with dried parts of oranges in them, and when I asked about these, I was told McDonalds used them to fill out their burgers and soak up excess moisture.

Already, the trip had taught me that there were so many by-products from oranges that we could gain value from. And this lesson did not end there. From Brazil, north to Florida and then onto California. Florida wasn't particularly enlightening but in California I saw how they turned orange peel into cattle food. So I came back with this incredible vision of what we could do back in Australia, things that had never been done before here.

My role of managing director basically meant I had to do everything from a management point of view. I had no sales or marketing people. I was the finance controller, the construction controller, and as the business grew, I took on the oversight of engineering and equipment. We started with a shed, a freezer and some basic equipment. I was ably assisted by Muzefa Pakravan, Nick Cavallo, Peter Noonan and Loris Davis.

There were some financially unstable times early on. The National Australia Bank was our financier and at one stage, between all the stock and other expenditure, we were running a bit short of money. The bank threatened to cancel our cheques, but I came up with an idea I hoped would cut that off at the pass. We needed $600 000, so I suggested I get our sixty members to each write a letter guaranteeing $10 000 if we lost the money. The members all agreed; they were confident the business was travelling well enough that they would not have to pay any of that guarantee. We got our $600 000 from the bank and it was all go from there.

Within ten years Murrayland Fruit Juices grew to a $45m turnover, employing 106 people. Our customers included Coca Cola, Cadbury Schweppes, Mr Juice and Sunpak; we had customers in Perth, Brisbane, all over Australia. Even the Governor-General paid us a visit.

One of the most interesting deals involved Glaxo, ex-manufacturer of Ribena. They wanted to create another product, which they called Vita-10, to put on the shelves next to Ribena. The problem was, they couldn't find anyone who could make what they wanted. They'd even approached the Mildura Co-Op. The product they wanted was to contain ten different fruits: orange, lemon, grapefruit, grapes, mango, passionfruit, mandarin, guava, pineapple and banana. Muzefa Pakravan, the Iranian chemist working for the business, told me he could make what they wanted, no problem. We ended up making 2000 x 200 litre drums, at 4:1 concentrate; some 400 000 litres.

Expansion of the business included buying the Nestlé factory in Merrigum, near Shepparton, in 1987, for processing apples and apple juice. The business bought Mildura Wine in Irymple, which was nearby, and invested an enormous amount in that. We installed twelve million litres of storage tanks, plus extra presses and filters, because we wouldn't have had enough capacity to keep up with the growth of the volume. We didn't make wine, we just processed grapes and sold the juice to Yalumba and other big wine companies to make their wine. That was a great business as well.

Unfortunately, with success comes jealousy, and much of it came from the members. Remember, they had invested just $7000 each at the beginning, but this had grown into hundreds of thousands of dollars, with great dividends every year. You would have thought they'd be happy but there were some who just questioned how much I was getting out of it, and claiming it wasn't deserved. I was away from my family two weeks in every month, travelling all over the country, selling, selling, selling, flying here and flying there, and then coming back and hearing whispers about my performance. When we received an offer for the business from the national food company, Southern Farmers, in 1989,

I recommended that members accept it. I had had enough. The members voted in favour and we sold the business for nearly $14.5m. The original sixty investors each received approximately $240 000 (and that doesn't include the annual dividends). It was quite a result for the time, at least, I think.

Popular Alm

Kilmore Cup, 1982

One of my passions, other than family and business, is horses, both thoroughbreds and pacers. It wasn't an interest I grew up with, but working in the restaurant business, it seemed that every second day, someone would ask if I was interested in buying a horse or a share in a horse.

The first time I succumbed to such an offer was in the early 1970s, when I still had Dominic's. Convinced by a friend to buy a share in a horse, we sent it to the legendary Colin Hayes to be trained. Colin trained more than 5000 winners in his career, but unfortunately this horse was not one of them. It only took Colin two months of handling the horse before he said, 'Don, this horse is not going to be any good.'

Despite this first negative experience in horse ownership being less than fruitful, in terms of wins and prizemoney, I was hooked. I even became a breeder of horses. That happened because Donata, when she was a teenager, decided she wanted a horse to ride, as teenagers are wont to do. And of course, as is common, her enthusiasm eventually waned. Rather than sell Donata's horse, I used her as a broodmare, sent her to a local stallion each season, and raced the offspring. This resulted in 27 wins from four different horses. Those wins were on local tracks, but there was one city winner with a horse I part-owned, Bella Art. I gave up buying into thoroughbreds after buying a yearling off Gerry Harvey. The horse was well bred, by Flying Spur, and the price tag reflected that. We discovered, however, that it had a crook heart, so we lost our money, and that was it for me, as far as thoroughbreds went. Anna would complain the whole hobby was a waste of money, but I could not see it from her perspective.

Pacers, or trotters as they are also known, were a completely different story. I was lucky enough to have a sizeable share in one of Australia's best-ever pacers, Popular

Alm (now honoured with an eponymous small court off Eleventh Street in Mildura). My involvement came about when Vin and Bob Knight, legends of the sport, saw this colt and decided, just from the look of him, that he could be special. They went about finding owners for it and sold shares to some friends of mine. When they still had 30% left to sell, they came to me; and with my friends already committed, I joined them. What a decision that was!

Popular Alm won 49 races and was placed 10 other times, from 61 starts. He won three Miracle Miles, two Italian Cups, and numerous others of the biggest races in Australian pacing. In fact, he won every Australian group-one race except the Inter Dominion in Perth. One night at Moonee Valley in 1983, he set a world record time trial of 1:53.2, for the "miracle mile"; and in 2009 he was inducted into the Victorian Harness Racing Hall of Fame, in its inaugural year.

Poppy, as he was known, gave us so many pleasures, and I still get goose bumps thinking of him racing, and of the doors that that horse opened for us. It was an unbelievable experience. What I would give for him to know our gratitude!

Riverside Village and Piccola Italia

The 1980s saw a consolidation of my business activities in Mildura, in a couple of very different ways. The first involved purchasing a 12 ½ acre property between Eighth and Twelfth Streets, facing Riverside Avenue. I subdivided five acres for housing between Eighth and Ninth Streets, naming a court Donmaria, after our daughters.

For the rest of the land, I had a vision for a retirement village, but it was a bit ahead of its time. In 1981/82, the first thirty-one units, a clubhouse, a pool and bowling green were built. The permit provided for up to 106 units, and that was certainly the plan. Anna played a large role in

this as well, furnishing and overseeing the interior design of each unit.

Don and Anna welcoming tennis champions to Riverside Village

Now this was a time of high interest rates, more than 20%. Add bank fees on top of that and repayments were close to 25% for money borrowed. In hindsight, it was the wrong time to embark on this dream project. When an opportunity came along to sell the property, I grabbed it. It came about when I saw an article in the local paper indicating investor interest in setting up a timeshare resort in Mildura. The investor was a businessman named Ken Buchanan and it was the ideal property for him. We had lunch and made a handshake deal that involved very little direct profit for me but a generous one million shares in the resort, on top of the purchase price. Today, the Sunraysia Resort is recognised as one of the best timeshares in Australia, running at an average

98% occupancy. Unfortunately, neither Ken nor I retained any ownership to benefit from its success; the high interest rates and large expenditure sent him into bankruptcy, and my shares went with it.

With the retirement home dream gone, my sights were set elsewhere. In 1985, my Italian heritage influenced the next business, which fell back onto two of my proven strengths, hospitality and development. Of course, there had been an Italian air around Mildura for several decades due to migration, but not like *Piccola Italia*, or Little Italy to the locals, a hospitality complex at the lower end of Deakin Avenue behind The Grand Hotel. It was opened by Don Dunstan, the former charismatic premier of South Australia. That came about because I met him on a trip to Japan when he was Director of Tourism for the State of Victoria. He knew of my involvement in hospitality and tourism and I told him, 'I've got a complex in Mildura I'd like you to open,' and he was thrilled to do so.

Underneath what was the original Chaffey Mildura Club was an incredible cellar with a steak house. Out the back, a garden restaurant. The complex included a small pasta and gelato business, selling fresh, take-away food. And there was a pizzeria. There were about thirty staff all-told, including half a dozen pizza makers. Once again, Anna was pivotal to this venture.

In 1989, the whole business was sold to three partners, but as usual, I kept the properties. It eventually closed down. The building is historic to Mildura, having housed *The Mildura*

Cultivator newspaper in the late 1800s, and being home to members of the famous Chaffey family (Mildura's founders). Much later, in 2000, Stefano de Pieri opened a café in part of the complex, aptly naming it '27 Deakin'.

Anna and I decided to donate one of the buildings, 29 Deakin Avenue, to La Trobe University. At the official handover of the building, I recall how good it felt to give back something substantial to the community, knowing I had arrived in Australia with nothing at all.

The Bellboy Comes Home

All the while I was running businesses, whatever they may have been, I never forgot it all started for me as a bellboy at The Grand Hotel. I couldn't have forgotten about The Grand. Not only was it the landmark building in Mildura, but so many of my businesses had been located near it. From the time I left there to open the Mary Elizabeth, there was hardly a day that I did not walk past The Grand which had left an indelible memory of those early days as a new arrival in Australia.

By 1986, when I had my hands full around the corner at *Piccola Italia*, The Grand had been bought by the Interwest Group, a large publicly listed company. Their ownership of The Grand was somewhat of a shemozzle. Remember, these were the the eighties when many businesspeople lost their heads. They grew their businesses quickly, and on the back of heavy debt. Interwest was no lightweight in the industry. At their peak they owned thirteen major hotels, including Club One and Gateway Hotel in Brisbane, Melbourne Chateau and Eden on the Park in Melbourne, and others in Sydney, Perth and New Zealand. Yet, as far as The Grand was concerned,

My Story: Living in Opportunity

they did not invest in the property after purchasing it. They didn't maintain it to the degree it needed to be maintained, didn't carry out repairs; they just treated it as a cash cow. Unfortunately, the revenue coming from it, as with all their hotels by the end of the eighties, was not even enough to cover their debt. In late 1989, Interwest was put into receivership and The Grand was put up for auction.

A month before the auction, I had sold Murrayland Fruit Juices, so I had cash on hand. The thought of buying The Grand appealed to me greatly. Firstly, what a story it would be: from bellboy to owner—the thought made me glow hot. Secondly, and more importantly, I had a passion for the place that the previous owners had not had. I knew what it meant for Mildura and I saw an opportunity to right a wrong; to restore the former jewel of the city to its rightful place.

As the auction neared, I spoke to a few people in the industry, including someone in Adelaide close to the company, Adelaide Steamship, which had helped Interwest buy The Grand, and which were still owed $5.5m. This source told me that Adelaide Steamship would be happy if The Grand was sold for just that amount: they weren't interested in a dollar more, just what they were owed.

On the day of the auction, instructions were given to the person bidding on my behalf. 'Have a look around and if no-one else bids first, start at $5m. If the auction hots up, go to five and a half, then stop.'

It didn't need to go to five and a half. No-one else bid, and we negotiated a price of $5.2m. On 14 December 1989, The Grand Hotel was mine, almost exactly thirty years since I had walked out of there to start my own business life.

You would have thought that having The Grand Hotel back in the hands of a local who loved the building and the city would have brought joy into the hearts of everyone in Mildura. Unfortunately, that wasn't the case, and that tall-poppy theme sadly resurfaced. For some of Mildura establishment, it was like a bullet had been put through their heart. They didn't consider me to be one of them.

Some had had a financial interest in the hotel for many years, and though they'd had plenty of opportunities to sell their shares, many held out for more and more. As a result of Interwest going into receivership, putting the hotel up for sale, and my buying it, they lost heavily on their investment in The Grand. Some came up to me and said things like, 'You bastard, you got our hotel for nothing.' It wasn't for nothing – I bought it with the accumulation of my life's and my family's work and sacrifices.

Then, of course, the rumours started.

'He's selling drugs.'

'How does he have that sort of money?'

'How much marijuana has this bloke sold to be able to spend five million dollars.'

What they didn't realise was that I had five million dollars from the sale of my business the month before. I was all cashed up and ready to go. I didn't have to borrow a single cent. I ignored the rumours and went about making The Grand a hotel that Mildura would again be proud of.

Over the next few years, some seven or eight million dollars was spent upgrading the hotel. In fact, we basically kept upgrading and developing the property for the next twenty years, a piece at a time (sorry to the guests for the constant nailing and drilling!). All of the bars were converted to restaurants; all of the rooms from poky little rooms to larger, opened up rooms. New plumbing, electrical wiring and modern telecommunications facilities were installed. I built the Ballroom, which has since hosted countless wedding receptions and major conferences.

The biggest battle in all the years I owned the hotel was over poker machines. In 1991, when poker machines were introduced to Victoria, The Grand was nominated as the first country hotel to get 105 machines when they were to be released. I was so excited—they were cause for that then. On the application, I put my manager down to be the nominee of the license. He had been a loyal employee.

What I didn't count on, although I had experienced it before, was the insistence of some influential people in this city to stop me succeeding. In a very short time, certainly before we had gone before the licencing board as part of our application, my manager resigned. He had been made an offer too good to refuse, to manage the Gateway Hotel on Fifteenth Street, the opposite end of town, which had just become the first hotel in about 70 years to be built in Mildura.

The reason it took so long for a hotel to be built in Mildura is interesting. In the 1880s, just after The Grand Hotel was built, the temperance movement became so strong in Mildura that ordinances were passed to prohibit any more hotels in the city. Clubs, for some reason, were allowed, even though they served alcohol. That's why the Mildura Workers Club, the Settlers Club, and the RSL, became large entities; there was no local competition. The Workers Club's main claim to fame was having the longest bar in the world, though, sadly, it has since been demolished to make way for poker machines.

So, the Gateway Hotel was built in 1989 at the end of the ban on off-premise licenses, my manager was poached a couple of years later, and I heard nothing about my application for poker machines. At The Grand, a room had been renovated for the machines with bases ready to go. Every now and again I would go down to the police station and ask for progress, only to be stonewalled. Clearly, there was a campaign against me. Then this saga took a very nasty turn.

One day, two police officers came into the hotel and asked me to accompany them to the police station.

'What for?' I asked.

'You either come voluntarily or you'll come in the divvy van,' was their response.

There was no point arguing but I insisted on driving myself there.

Sitting at an interview table, I was accused of sexually harassing my staff. I was flabbergasted.

'I've been in this business since I was 19,' I told them. 'And I've had more women around me than you've got hairs in your bloody head. There is no way I have ever harassed or abused any of them.'

They insisted I answer to the allegations, but I told them I wouldn't do so without my solicitor. At that point, they told me they had enough information and there would not be any need for further questions. However, their demeanour suggested this would not be the end of the matter.

Shortly after, I was told I would not be getting the machines I had applied for. Word travelled fast, or others knew in advance, because almost as soon as I was informed, I got a phone call from the guy who had installed the bases for me, asking when he could come over and pick them up. I assumed they were wanted elsewhere. I was left with an empty room, no machines, and, worst of all, no official explanation as to why. I tried to get the official report on my application, but the relevant government department would not release it to me.

Owning the largest hotel in a large rural city meant I got to meet, and become friends with, many influential people. One of those was Brian Bourke, celebrated Victorian barrister, who had represented Ronald Ryan, the last person hanged in Victoria. I gave him a call. 'Something's wrong here,' I told him. 'Somebody wants to block me.' I filled him in on the poker machine debacle and the allegations, and pleaded, 'You've got to do something about it.'

'Leave it to me,' he said.

After a couple of weeks, Brian got back to me and said, 'They're not going to release any report until the court case.'

'What court case?' I asked.

'They're going to take you to court over the allegations of sexual harassment.'

I couldn't believe it. 'Brian, for God's sake,' I yelled down the phone, 'I haven't done anything wrong. I haven't touched anybody.'

He told me to be careful, that there were obviously people out to ruin me.

Eventually, the court case came around. There were media cameras outside. I walked in with Anna, who was as solid as a rock in supporting me. As soon as we were inside, Brian called us aside and said, 'You've got a female judge. That's not going to work in your favour.'

I got worried because the trial was by judge, not jury, so Brian's warning was to be taken seriously. Then he added, 'If I can get a deal whereby you plead guilty without any judgement against you, take it.'

'No way. I don't want a deal. I've done nothing wrong.'

Brian insisted it was the best way forward, but I stood firm.

The case started and one of the women who had made allegations against me was called to give evidence. Brian asked her exactly what I had done to her. She claimed that when she walked past me, I had tapped her on the shoulder. Under further questioning, she said I did that to many people, and admitted it was probably because of my European nature.

The witness was then asked why she had brought charges against me. Her response was to go red in the face. At that moment I knew that she had been coerced to make the allegations, but she stuck firm.

During a break, Brian again advised me to plead guilty, that the judge would likely rule against me. Again, I refused.

'Don,' he said firmly. 'You've employed me as your advisor, I'm giving you advice. Plead guilty, no conviction, and you're home and hosed.'

By now, Anna was on Brian's side. She could see the sense of his argument. 'Do what Brian tells you.' So I pleaded guilty to a couple of minor charges.

A month later, the report into my poker machine application was released and a determination had been made that the hotel would receive twenty machines to be managed by my wife and my daughters alone. Twenty machines, out of the 105 I had originally been led to believe were to come. I found out that among those who opposed my application were a leading figure in the National Party in the region, and a director of the other hotel. Their campaign against me cost tens of millions of dollars over the years, but more importantly, it stopped the people of Mildura having an entertainment and gaming complex like nothing they would have experienced—certainly nothing that has been created since, what with a hotel incorporating 100 rooms, a swimming pool, gym, two bottleshops, a bistro, a cellar restaurant, several bars and function spaces. The wound from those allegations and the corruption is still smarting.

What these experiences did do was harden me for other times, one of which, and I will get to that later, makes this one almost pale into insignificance.

But back to the positives of The Grand Hotel, because it is positives I like to focus on. One of my initiatives at The Grand Hotel, designed to boost Mildura's tourism profile even higher, was the creation of the Mildura Quality Wine Centre at the hotel in 1998. The centre incorporated an upstairs tasting room overlooking the hotel's courtyard and pool, and a temperature-controlled wine gallery. It provided opportunities for local winemakers to showcase their product to locals and tourists.

The hotel was a monster of a set-up, and very much a family affair. Anna oversaw all purchases, organised staff rosters and took care of all the decorative touches. Maria ran front reception, while Donata and her husband, Stefano, set up and ran the cellar restaurant. Down the track, Maria's husband, Mario, ran the pizza café on Langtree Avenue. We worked together every day and loved it. Furthermore, it created a real buzz in town.

In 1999 and 2000, the family efforts in restoring The Grand Hotel were officially recognised. In 1999 the Australian Hotels Association presented me with the Nick Nikakis Memorial Award for my "focus on developing and improving hotels, through training to ensure consistency in areas of food service, décor and entertainment, emphasising the ever-increasing high standards of the industry". The following year at the prestigious Diners Club International Australian Hotels' Association National Awards for Excellence the hotel was noted for Best Mid-Range Accommodation and Best Prestigious Dining Venue. About the same time, rumours swirled around Mildura that I was selling the hotel. What a lot of nonsense. Those rumours had cropped up a few times over the years but this time they were louder and more persistent. I don't know what the motivations were for such rumours but everywhere I went I was asked about them. There was even a front-page story about the rumours in the Sunraysia Daily, and at least that afforded me the opportunity to dismiss them to a large readership.

In 2002, Anna and I decided to relinquish some of the workload, and so restructured the management of the hotel, in effect splitting it into four distinct areas, but all still part of The Grand Hotel business. There was the Pizza Café and Barbecue Lane, managed by my brother's children, Joseph and Lina; the TAB, saloon bar, drive-through bottle shop and gaming room, managed by Maria and her husband, Mario; Stefano's restaurant, managed by Donata and her husband Stefano de Pieri; and all the accommodation, conferencing and other hotel operations, to be managed by a general manager. The ownership structure remained the same, and Anna and I were still very much involved but I had more time to focus on other endeavours, including within the community.

In 2006, I received an offer for the hotel that was worth considering. So worthwhile, in fact, that I accepted it. It was only the hotel business that was sold, indeed, leased for twenty years. Anna and I remained owners of the property, and the areas of the business managed by my family members stayed in their hands. Unfortunately, the hotel business went into receivership due to circumstances beyond Mildura, and out of control of the owners (a pity because they were good operators), and in 2009 the receivers sold the lease to the Quality Hotel chain.

*

Over the past thirty or so years, when people think of Mildura, many of them think of food, wine, and hospitality. That wasn't always the case. Three people, in particular, are responsible for that perception, and, as a result, putting Mildura on the foodie and entertaining map. Yes, I was partly responsible, through the ownership of several hospitality establishments, as were other local businesses, but my daughter, Donata, and her husband, Stefano de Pieri, can claim an enormous amount of the credit. The main reason was the screening of the ABC television series called *A Gondola on the Murray* that aired from 1998 featuring Stefano as host in a Mildura setting. The program went world-wide and was repeated, and continues to be to this day, now on the SBS food channel.

I first met Stefano in 1989, when Donata brought him up from Melbourne to meet us. Anna and I welcomed him into the family with open arms. Shortly after, they announced they were going to get married. Stefano's mother was too frail to fly to Australia from Italy, so the decision was made to have the wedding in Italy. It wasn't a tough decision. We have so many relatives there ourselves, and few of them travel to Australia. This way we could could catch up with them, and the de Pieri and Carrazza families could all meet each other.

So, in June 1991, we flew to Italy for Donata and Stefano's wedding. It was held at Villa Condulmer in Mogliano, Veneto, not far from the area where Stefano's family hails. The villa was unbelievable. The stables had been converted into luxurious guest rooms, and the restaurant reflected the rest of the property, a touch of the old and worldly, and a touch of the modern and innovative. Apparently, the composer Giuseppe Verdi used to stay at the villa, and

Ronald and Nancy Reagan had stayed there on the occasion of a gathering of the G7.

Anna and I arrived the day before the wedding, and throughout the afternoon our relatives from the south of Italy and from Australia checked in. To celebrate such a rare gathering, I booked a restaurant for dinner for everyone. We had an absolute ball because we hadn't met any of Stefano's family before then. It set the tone for a couple of days of feasting and celebration. The only problem came at the end of that dinner when I went to pay the bill with my credit card.

'I'm afraid we don't take this card,' the owner said.

After a bit of toing and froing, we agreed that we would meet at the bank the next morning and I would withdraw the cost of the dinner in cash for him.

The wedding was magnificent, everything we had hoped it would be. Much of the credit goes to Stefano's brother, Sergio, who organised it all. Over the years, Sergio became as much a part of the family as Stefano, dividing his life between Italy and Australia.

After the wedding, we drove south to spend time with members of our family who hadn't come up for the wedding, and, of course, to introduce them to Stefano. From there we went to Naples, Rome, London, then home. But, when in Naples, I took Stefano for a drink in the lobby of the hotel and I said to him 'Why don't you ditch your political ambitions and come and help us in Mildura? I know you already have a passion for food and beverage. You can do anything you like, perhaps even television.' Stefano always asked me where the hell I got that idea from and I must confess I don't even know myself, but it came true. Sometimes you win the lottery!

Donata and Stefano returned to Melbourne after they married, and Stefano had ambitions to enter politics. He had always been involved in politics, and worked as a political adviser, but he had eyes for something bigger. Unfortunately, internal Labor Party shenanigans stymied his moves, pissing Stefano off no end.

By late 1990 Stefano and Donata joined us in Mildura. Two things happened at that time. The first was the opening of a large bottleshop in what is now the Pizza Café. The second was my idea of opening an eatery in the old cellar of The Grand Hotel.

At first, everyone thought I was crazy. 'Who in the world is going to go down there,' they said. And who could blame them, it looked terrible. Dark, dank, smelly due to poor drainage and being the home to some other less-romantic internal plumbing. No-one could envisage what we were able to turn it into.

It took an enormous effort to create a space for dining and cooking. In some places along the passageway, it was only five-foot-five high. So, we had to dig, and do all sorts of renovations to make it comply with regulations. Putting in a staircase was a nightmare. Even after all that work, we were forced to close soon after we had opened because authorities realised we only had one exit. Fair enough, I guess. It would have been dangerous in a case of fire. So, we cut open another exit, making enormous quantities of rubble, noise and dust during the night, and we were back in business.

And what a business it has been. Stefano's, as the restaurant is called, has been virtually booked out every night since we opened. It has had a huge impact on Mildura. In tourism terms, it's not unlike the effect MONA has had on Hobart, albeit on a smaller scale.

From the outset, one of the things that helped get word around was not having a menu. I told Stef, 'Let's not have a menu. Just give people what is good each day. They'll love it and they'll come back.' And it worked. We started very simply, like a small café, with antipasto, crusty bread and a variety of pasta. We would serve a platter with three different pastas.

My experience in hospitality had taught me that you never get a complaint if you serve people quickly. But you get a hell of a lot of complaints if you keep them waiting. So, I told Stef and the staff, 'If we can create an image of good service, of fast turnaround, we'll never go wrong.'

The Stefano's Restaurant experience began the moment guests walked in. Donata and Stefano worked solidly together, she in front-of-house, training staff and delivering service while Stefano oversaw food and wine choices and the necessities of the kitchen. We placed a blackboard just inside the door, on which was chalked the antipasto and pasta that was available that day. One day we might have gnocchi, one day we might have cannelloni, one day we might have ravioli; the emphasis was on service and freshness.

As good and simple as this venture was, it was destined to change. That change came about after Stefano hosted the TV series, *Gondola on the Murray* in the late 1990s. Suddenly the town was awash with tourists from all over Australia, and of course, they wanted to go to Stefano's. This was at the end of the 1990s and early 2000s: the reputation of the restaurant soared, and the awards and accolades flowed our way. In the early 2000s, Stefano's was one of the must-visit restaurants in Australia. Donata and Stefano developed their skills much like me, through doing the work and learning along the way.

In the early 1980s, Stefano worked for a short time for Melbourne chef Raymond Fenech, but he never formally trained as a chef, and still refuses to use that title, preferring to be labelled a cook. However, he has unbelievable dedication and devotion, and has always met the challenges thrown at him. We brought in some Italian chefs over time, and I believe panna cotta was introduced to Australia through them so new ideas were always flowing in.

Stefano stepped out of the business for a couple of years in 2014–16, and the restaurant was taken over by two employees, but his sabbatical was short-lived when the dreams and ideas of the new owners failed to be realised, and Stefano again took over. It remains a tourism magnet for Mildura, and one of the most appealing restaurants in the country.

But I have raced ahead of time in telling this story. Soon after the underground restaurant was established with people being able to purchase wine to bring downstairs to consume with their meal, Stefano also saw an opportunity to serve some food in the bottleshop itself. He took the initiative, placed a small table amongst the boxes of wine, and started to serve a bit of salami. It was a distinctly European touch but it took off. One table became two tables, then three, until we relocated the pizzeria from inside the hotel to this new site and it became the Pizza Café.

Next to The Grand Hotel is a property that had, for many years, housed retail shops and businesses, including a Harvey World Travel agency, the Boomerang bookshop and a barber. Behind it was a perpetually steaming laundry for the hotel (these were the days before external linen companies), a workshop, and a carpark. I bought the property in 1989, with the intention of creating an entertainment venue, the focal point of which would be the poker machines I had expected to receive a licence for.

For some time, the spaces in front were leased out to businesses, but the majesty of the main art deco building, formally the Astor Theatre, demanded more, far more. It was there hiding under pigeon droppings and years of black dust, and I put a great deal of thought into identifying what the space could best be used for. The idea that came up was to convert the space into a micro-brewery. There were two companies, CUB and Tooheys, controlling nearly 20 billion dollars' worth of business, and I felt that even grabbing some of the crumbs that were left would be worthwhile. In addition, it fitted my interest in hospitality; it was right next door to The Grand and would be another boost to Mildura's tourism industry.

The Mildura Brewery opened on 10 December 2004, at a time when there were few micro-breweries in Australia. Among those at the opening was John Anderson, then deputy prime minister. Getting to the point of opening was quite an effort. The renovation was massive. We basically gutted everything. The architect was John Mantesso of Interlandi Mantesso Architects. John was my go-to architect for many developments, particularly at The Grand. I first showed him the building that was to house the brewery in 1992, and we discussed options for a decade before going full bore.

The Honourable John Anderson AO, Julia Robertson, Don and Anna

Of course, the building was only one part of what became another great business. The beer had to be good as well. To ensure the quality and uniqueness of our beer Stephen Nelsen was appointed as master brewer. Stephen had worked in the industry in Australia, Britain and Europe, and when he was offered the job, he considered it was like getting a new toy.

I certainly made sure Stephen had all the equipment he needed. There were five double-sized fermenters and two enormous bright beer tanks; the combination of which had the capacity to pump out tonnes of bottles a year.

The first beers in the range were the Desert Premium Lager, Mallee Bull, Murray Honey Wheat and Sun Light. Our beers won 20 medals at the 2005 Australian International Beer Awards with Sun Light named Best Beer in its category. It was a reward for the efforts of so many people. Over the years, we added to the range, often with seasonal brews.

Within months, we secured almost thirty Melbourne outlets, and others in regional Victoria. In 2006, we appointed Neqtar Wines & Beverages to be the sole distributor of our beer, ensuring even wider national distribution. In 2007, we received our first order from Italy, for a brew under the export label, True Blue Lager. Selling beer to Italy was obviously of enormous personal satisfaction but what it showed, more than anything else, was that the local Mildura product was as good as any.

The front-of-house of the brewery business began under the management of Joseph Carrazza, my nephew, followed by Mario, my son-in-law. After some permutations, the whole complex was operated by Donata and Stefano for five years. The Mildura Brewery was always much more than just about beer. Stefano, who also helped develop the beers, managed the food outlets while Donata ran front-of-house. We had developed a small precinct, based around The Grand Hotel, Stefano's and Mildura Brewery, that you would not have found the like of in any other Australian rural town or city—of that I am certain.

In 2017, we sold the brewery. Stefano and Donata were busy with other interests and I didn't want to continue without them. We sold the brand as well. Looking back, I take enormous satisfaction out of what was achieved. I spent millions bringing back an Art Deco building from a state of disrepair. We kept aspects of the original theatre, so locals could come and reminisce. And, from scratch, the lot of us created a unique brewery from which award-winning, world-class beers were produced. Who wouldn't be proud of that?

Mildura's Unrealised Jewel

A ROYAL WELCOME

Page from prospectus

Everything I have done in business, every development, every venture, would have paled into insignificance if the project I consider to be Mildura's unrealised jewel was realised. It was a project that would have transformed this city into one of Victoria's great regional tourist destinations. It would have created so much employment and economic activity. Yet again, a combination of conflicting opinions and unjustified fears, and perhaps a bit of malice, saw that the project would not go ahead. I am talking about a vision for a casino in Mildura. Worth the gamble?

The idea presented itself not long after purchasing the land across the road from The Grand Hotel on Seventh Street. It was used as a car park, mainly for guests at The Grand, but I considered it wasted space. When local authorities began talking about a river development in front of the hotel, my brain clicked into action. Some local consultants started drawing up plans, and costing a development, and it ran into millions of dollars—much of it, potentially, at public expense. I started making other plans, considering what I could do that would create jobs, be a long-term asset for the city, and not cost the taxpayer a cent. A casino came to mind: a multifaceted entertainment, elegant accommodation and function complex for conferences that would attract business from out of town. More poker machines were the last thing that I had in mind. Mildura was already serviced on both sides of the river by hundreds of machines operating seven days a week into the night. I really had in mind something highly sophisticated for Mildura for an international clientele.

When it comes to casinos and entertainment in Australia, no one knows more than John Haddad. He got the first casino licence in Australia, for Wrest Point Casino in Hobart, and is in the Australian Hotels Association (AHA) Hall of Fame. We were both on the AHA Council and I said to him privately, 'There's an opportunity for a second casino in Victoria and it couldn't be better than Mildura. We are so far away from Melbourne. There is no competition either way.'

'Yes,' said John, 'it makes sense.'

Then he asked if I had a place to build it. Did I have a place! The car park was perfect. I told John, all I needed him to do was find some investors.

So, we got to work. First, we appointed architects to consider the idea. They were mighty impressed. Then they got the ideas down on paper, so people could make sense of the vision.

While all this was going on, we had a couple of meetings with John Brumby, who was premier of Victoria at the time. Obviously, government approval would make or break the project. After hearing us out and looking at our plans, he said, 'You certainly have the right place. Mildura is a long way from Melbourne, so if you guys have got the facilities, I'll sign off on it.' There was, however, one condition. The opposition also had to agree. Gambling and casinos were issues on which there was no general agreement in framing policies. John Brumby did not want political controversies at the next election.

The next step was to talk to the National and Liberal parties. I was sure I wasn't going to have any problems with the National Party, after all, they support just about everything in Mildura and, at that time, had a political hold on the place. Why would they object? I also thought the Liberal Party would be a piece of cake. They usually bowed to their coalition partner up here. So, we made an appointment with the Liberal leader, Ted Baillieu, and the National leader, Peter Ryan, presented our idea, showed them our plans, and they also indicated firm approval. Even former premier, Jeff Kennett, claimed Mildura was the perfect location for a second casino in Victoria. It was onwards and upwards.

We completed designs and plans, made a small, to-scale model of the casino complex—which cost me about thirty grand alone—and in 2010 we set up a display at the local tourism centre. It blew the locals away. The display was up for three months, during which time objections could be made.

Why were they so blown away? Well, let me take you through the complex. It was to be a $400m entertainment centre and casino, with conference facilities, a hotel, and concert and theatre spaces. The largest conference hall would have held 1000 people, seated. And it was to be called the Mildura Jewel.

In Victoria, State elections are held on the last Saturday of November every four years. There was one due on 27 November 2010. I did not give much thought to the upcoming election, at least not in relation to the casino proposal that was now taking up most of my waking time. After all, whoever won would support the project, and the losers wouldn't oppose it. What a position to be in.

About two months before the election, the tide turned. Until then, I had no indication that anything would go amiss. What I didn't know is that some of the clubs in the Mildura area, fearful for their survival if the casino was built, had started lobbying the Liberal and National parties, knowing they only had to sway them, and the casino would probably be 'dead in the water', so-to-speak. My understanding is that both Ted Baillieu and Peter Ryan, and certainly other officials of the parties, were told they could expect no support in the upcoming election unless they changed their mind. Both parties succumbed to the pressure and reversed their position on the casino. They weren't thinking about what such an enterprise would do for the region; they weren't thinking how Mildura would be transformed; they were thinking only of political advantage.

I don't blame Ted Baillieu so much; in fact I believe he wanted to remain supportive. It was Peter Ryan and the National Party, particularly their local member for Mildura, Peter Crisp, who became so fearful they would lose this seat if they supported the casino because there was some vocal opposition from local stakeholders.

We didn't take it lying down. We backed an independent candidate, Doug Tonge, in the election. We provided signs, which were plastered around the electorate, we door knocked in specially made shirts, a costly campaign. He ended up with almost 15% of the vote, an amazing effort for a first time, but the Nationals won, and the clubs came calling, wanting their reward for backing Peter Crisp. The casino was dead and a large swathe of the town was broken hearted; only the clubs rejoiced. Of course, there was opposition from a section of the public, but supporters of the casino regarded that as hypocritical. There are still hundreds of poker machines in town.

I cannot overstate how important the casino would have been for Mildura. The city would be a completely different one than it is now. For one thing, unemployment would be a good deal lower; the employment opportunities, particularly for young people, would have been amazing. Tourists would be flocking into Mildura all year round. The airport would have been upgraded. Even today, I am regularly stopped in the street and told, 'Don, we're so sorry we didn't see that beautiful complex go ahead because it looked spectacular.' Those people didn't forget. I am pleased the National party lost its seat at the next election.

I ended up selling that car park, as the disappointment was just too much. I couldn't think of how else to develop it. My heart wouldn't have been in it.

Creating Jobs (Real Jobs)

Don, Employee of the Month recipient Casey Clark, Bill Carroll, Kris Harrington

In 1995, Prime Minister Paul Keating announced that he wanted to give Australia's rural regions greater autonomy to manage their own affairs. He divided the country into 56 regions, one of which was Mildura and its immediate surrounds, in both Victoria and NSW. Organisations called Area Consultative Committees (ACC) were formed in each region, and I was asked by Ken Carr, secretary of the local trade union council, to chair the one named Sunraysia Area Consultative Committee. It was a voluntary position, but I wasn't going to do it for the money anyway, it was an opportunity to give something back to a region I had benefitted from and which I loved.

As chair, I was responsible for choosing fourteen local people to join me on the Committee. I made sure they represented a range of views and sectors, including education, health, agriculture, business and engineering, and all had a passion for helping the region.

The ACCs all had the same brief, but I took the concept one step further than anyone envisaged. Within Victoria and Tasmania there were fifteen ACCs. After about a year of doing our own thing, I invited all the chairs of the fifteen to The Grand Hotel to meet and share what they'd been doing. As a result, we decided to continue the practice, and all meet in a different region, hosted by the relevant ACC, and continue to swap ideas. We also invited government ministers and guest speakers. Eventually we even had one such meeting in Canberra at Parliament House.

The main aim of the ACC was to help people find long-term work. That meant working with employers, local government, as well as those within the community who needed assistance. We wanted to get people off the dole, permanently. This would be done by providing both employment and training opportunities.

The first major project we undertook was a development of the Australian Inland Botanic Gardens in Mourquong, NSW. This was the first semi-arid botanical gardens in the southern hemisphere, and I got thirty people subsidised by the federal government to enhance the gardens. A bus would pick them up and drop them home, and within six months we had transformed the place.

As that was coming to an end (though we did continue to provide some labour at the gardens), we had already started looking ahead. This was the perfect opportunity to re-trellis some of the vineyards in the area. Most of our vines were very low to the ground and, as a result, little could be done mechanically. But with subsidised labour we lifted the trellises for mechanical harvesting. One hundred and twenty people were appointed to different growers, with the growers overseeing the labourers, and at the same time having their vineyards developed for the future.

The initiatives went on and on and have continued to this day. In the early years they included supporting apprentices in the engineering sector, online learning through Sunraysia TAFE, business and general life advice for young people, equipment for sports clubs, local infrastructure projects, managing issues around the Murray-Darling, and many more. We hosted many guest speakers, none more inspirational than ultra-marathon runner, Tony Rafferty.

One of the most important initiatives was kick-starting wider awareness of mental health issues. This started in about 1998 when ACC executive officer, Mark Wilson, said to me, 'We have so many suicides in Australia, but nobody knows or does anything about it.'

I swung into action and told Mark to find out who the best people in Australia were to get data from. As a result, I invited experts from five universities - Melbourne, La Trobe, Monash, Sydney and Flinders - to The Grand to meet with the ACC board. We told them how concerned we were with suicide rates and went through the data they had on suicide statistics, and other areas around mental health. We assured them that we would start lobbying for more action.

Straight after the meeting I got on the phone to the Victorian premier, Jeff Kennett, and told him about that discussion. He asked for the details which we sent. The next thing I heard, he had gone to Canberra and briefed Prime Minister John Howard about Australia's high suicide rates and demanded federal funds to help deal with the situation. In 2000, after losing the State election, he helped found and became chair of Beyond Blue, the main non-profit organisation in Australia, working to address issues associated with depression, suicide, anxiety disorders and other related mental disorders. But at no point did he ever acknowledge where the impetus for his interest in this area came from.

One day, several years later, he visited Mildura with his wife, Felicity. I had a cup of coffee with them and wasn't backward in telling him 'I thought you'd have the decency to say it started in Mildura. Not to mention my name, but to mention Sunraysia Area Consultative Committee, particularly as it's funded by the federal government.' That's politicians for you. I'm so proud of how we got that whole thing started, even if we don't get credit for it.

Without a doubt, the biggest achievement for the Sunraysia ACC has been its success in boosting Indigenous employment. This started in 2003 but almost collapsed in 2007. This is how: In 2003, I went to Canberra and said to the relevant minister, though I can't now remember who he was, 'I want to start an Indigenous employment program. Where can I get the funds from?' He said, 'The funds shouldn't be a problem. If you can find the jobs, we'll fund the employer without any problem. There's a special section for that in one of our programs.'

So, in 2003, our organisation started the Indigenous Employment Program with funding from the Department of Employment and Workplace Relations. The aim was to find 100 full-time jobs for local Indigenous people within three years. Employee of the month and employee of the year awards were instigated for those placed in jobs. In 2005, I was asked to present a talk on the success of our program at the annual national Area Consultative Committee chairs conference. We were the only ACC with such a program, and I outlined how the program was making a significant difference within our community.

Whether or not other ACCs would have taken up the challenge and formed their own versions is unknown; they never got the chance. In 2007, the newly elected prime minister, Kevin Rudd, abolished the ACCs. It was outrageous, and again we weren't going to take it sitting down. I immediately went to Canberra and spoke to some public servants about how I could maintain the Indigenous Employment Program. I asked one of them, 'Can I form a not-for-profit organisation with the stamp of the government so that I can still continue this?', and he responded, 'Put it all in writing and we'll deal with it.' In the end, I only had to tinker a little with our organisational structure. We have been operating the Indigenous Employment Program, under the banner of Sunraysia Regional Consulting since 2003, and so while Sunraysia ACC disappeared, we were able to keep Sunraysia Regional Consulting going. That's how the program has remained in existence to this day, while the work of the other 56 ACCs sadly has been pretty much forgotten.

That's not to say there haven't been roadblocks since then. From time to time, federal governments have changed contract and funding arrangements, which has been very frustrating. Whenever that occurred, I used whatever methods were available to pressure governments to come through with the goods. In January 2016, for example, we made the media aware that our future viability was threatened because we had not received funding commitments beyond the end of the year. A few months later, we received $1.045m for 100 new subsidised employments positions. The following year, we received a further $1.7m. In 2019, the federal government announced a new three-year commitment to our program. You need to know how to play the game—sitting around and hoping for favourable outcomes rarely works.

The organisation has been well served over the years by many dedicated people giving their time voluntarily and others who have worked in paid positions to ensure the success of the program. Our program has found employment for hundreds of Indigenous people, many of them young. While the jobs start off as subsidised positions, more than 60% of them convert to on-going, non-subsidised jobs.

To help promote the initiative, particularly in the media, we introduced an employee of the month award, which came with a $200 reward. We have kept many of the newspaper articles about these monthly winners and they show the breadth of the employment opportunities the program has catered for. Winners have come from the aged care sector, hospitality, nursery and gardening, transport, energy, health, engineering, and so many more.

In 2003, we went further and introduced an employee of the year award, with a formal function held in the ballroom of The Grand Hotel. More than 250 people attended the event, and we sent invites to the Indigenous elders, government ministers, and, of course, participants and nominees in the scheme—both employers and employees.

One of these events provided me with one the most gratifying moments I have had as chair of Sunraysia Regional Consulting, indeed, one of the most satisfying moments of my life. I was being the good host, moving from table to table making sure everyone was enjoying themselves, when I came to a table with one of the elders. I asked her if she was enjoying herself, and she told me, 'Mr Carrazza, I just want to thank you for what you do for us.'

I said, 'I'm really not doing anything. I'm only trying to employ some of the kids.'

She continued, 'Only a little over 10 years ago, we couldn't even put a foot in The Grand. We couldn't walk in The Grand. We couldn't go and buy a beer at the bar. And here we are in the ballroom, all the elders, beautifully dressed.' Now, if that doesn't show how worthwhile the program has been, nothing will.

Not every opportunity I provided to someone came through the bureaucratic organisational route. One stands out above most others, and that was a truck driver named Don Matthews. He worked for us transporting grapes when Dad and I were collecting them for the Italians in Melbourne. We only needed the truck for about three months a year, and I could see how passionate and loyal Don was. He couldn't afford to buy his own truck, so I let him take over the lease of the one he used when driving for us, and in return I made him promise that for the three months when I needed him, I would be his number one customer.

I had the kind of belief in Don's character that Mr Vance had shown in me so many years before. He expanded his business throughout the eighties and beyond, and his GTS Freight Management is one of the largest logistic transport companies in Australia today. I think they transport about 300 truckloads of stuff each day. Don's son, Damien, runs the business now, but it all started with that offer he accepted. I think about it whenever a GTS truck goes past on the highway.

Serving the Community

Many of the voluntary positions I have held, such as Sunraysia ACC and Sunraysia Regional Consulting were based around business and economic development. However, I am proud to have served the communities in and around Mildura in many other ways, particularly in sport and the arts.

My local sporting passion has been the Irymple Football Club. Like most regional areas, there are a number of football clubs in the Sunraysia. Why did I choose Irymple, some kilometres from where we grew up? Well, it goes back to the week I arrived in Mildura. Living next to my father's house in Buronga was an Australian family, and they had a daughter the same age as me. They also had an Austin car. The father had played football for Irymple and every Saturday during the football season, their family would pile into the Austin and go to watch Irymple play. On the first Saturday after my arrival, the neighbour asked my father if I could come along and watch, and Dad thought it was a great idea.

We got to the grounds and they had a special spot where they always sat, on a slope. I looked out at the oval expecting to see a goal with nets. But there were no nets, just four poles sticking up in the air, and I didn't know what the hell they were. Then, next thing I see these men running onto the oval holding and kicking these funny-shaped balls. And asking for clarification was out of the question, because I couldn't speak English.

It got more bizarre from there. When the match started, they grabbed the ball by their hands, and I had no idea why the referee didn't penalise them. On and on it went, my confusion growing.

I continued to go to matches, and slowly, both my English language skills and my knowledge of football improved. Years later, once I got into business, I got heavily involved with the Irymple Football Club. I was on their committee for 21 years, was president in 1987, and am their number one ticket holder.

The year I was president was a tumultuous one. The club had been left with some mismanagement from previous committees, most notably around a contract with the local council that specified we needed to pay Council some $160 000 for extensions and upgrade work. We did not have that sort of money, far from it, and I had to negotiate an agreement or else the club could have folded. Fortunately, that disaster was averted.

One of my philosophies, both as a committee member and president, was to develop young players. Many country clubs, like suburban clubs, raise money and buy more experienced players. This might bring short-term success (though it often doesn't work), but it is to the long-term detriment of the club and the community, and I vowed I would not go down that path.

One of Irymple's most successful fundraising events was the night I invited Allen Aylett, president/chairman of the North Melbourne Football Club, up to the club, and I got every one of the footballers to dress up as waiters and serve. So many people said it wouldn't work but boy it did. I think it was the wives and girlfriends who dragged their men along. After all, the footballers had great physiques and they were going to be serving drinks and food all night. The club and the district hadn't seen anything quite like it.

My other football passion has been the Carlton Football Club. My support for Carlton started in 1957 when I was working as a bellboy at The Grand. Carlton travelled to Mildura to play a pre-season practice match and the players all stayed at hotel. At the time, Carlton had three or four players who had Italian heritage, one of them being the famous Sergio 'Serge' Silvagni, who died in July 2021. Serge asked me who I barracked for, and when I told him 'no-one', he said, 'Well, you're a good little Italian boy, you should barrack for Carlton.' I've been a Carlton supporter ever since.

Funnily, I ended up with a strong connection to his family. Serge's son, another Carlton club legend, Steve Silvagni, married Jo Bailey. Jo's dad was a travelling salesman for a pharmaceutical company. He would stay in Mildura a lot and we became firm friends, dining together almost every time he was here.

Too often in Australia, people are deemed to be either sports or arts enthusiasts. The gap is probably more pronounced in rural communities, but I am proud to say I tread both paths. I love sport, particularly football and horse racing, but have supported many of the arts events and festivals that Mildura is now renowned for.

My contribution to the arts in Mildura dates back to 1962 when I held an art exhibition in the Mary Elizabeth. I contacted local artists and got them to exhibit works for sale, then set about the catering. In those days, catering at an art exhibition meant handing around sherry, and biscuits with little red onions topped with a bit of yellow cheese. Without that, you wouldn't get people in!

Since then, I have helped fund and raise money for the Mildura Wentworth Arts Festival, music festivals, the Mildura Arts Centre and many more. I am particularly proud of the development of the Mildura Writers Festival, which Donata and Stefano have been heavily involved with. It started in 1995 and is one of the premier writers' festivals in Victoria, if not Australia.

For many years, the patron of the Mildura Writers Festival was Les Murray, arguably Australia's greatest poet, and a bit of a larrikin. One morning, when he was down for the festival, he asked if he could borrow my car to look around the area. I had recently bought Anna a red Jaguar and, as Les was Australian literary royalty, threw him the keys to that car. After all, I didn't expect him to drive too far.

He disappeared for the day and when he came back late in the afternoon, the car was covered in dust and sounding very rattly. He had driven all the way to Mungo National Park, almost a two hour drive each way, a lot of it on rough, dusty roads. I wasn't game to tell Anna what had happened to her car, so I got the porters at The Grand to give it a good wash, and I then parked it at home as if nothing had happened. All would have been fine except that a couple of days later Les told Anna about his expedition to Mungo, including how he got there. That, they tell me, is what Les would call *The Quality of Sprawl*. Apparently, he wrote a poem about a man turning his Rolls Royce into a farm truck—lucky Les didn't go that far!

There have been a range of non-arts or sports initiatives and organisations that I have been associated with over the years. The Lions Club is one. What would a community be without its Lions Club? My club is the Buronga Gol Gol Lions Club and they are famous miles around for their steak sandwiches. I know making and selling steak sandwiches is not the main purpose of a Lions Club but over the years, the steak sandwiches we devised became almost folklore around here. The secret lay in tenderising the meat, heating the bread on the grill, and splitting the steak. We would sell six or seven thousand of these steak sandwiches at the local show each October.

In 2001, a Mildura-based organisation called Chances for Children grabbed my attention and I was happy to support it. It provides financial support to young people, who without help from Chances, may not have had the opportunity to pursue their education or maximise their talents and opportunities in sport or the arts.

Don and Anna Carrazza were yesterday presented with a plaque by Chances for Children chairman Eddie Warhurst in recognition of their continuing support for the youth project.

Sunraysia Daily, Saturday, June 22, 2002

Sometimes I have contributed to the community through what some considered to be hare-brained schemes. I thought they were just common sense.

One of them involved revitalising Deakin Avenue during a water shortage. Now, there are few, if any, places in

Australia, where water is more important than Mildura. The Murray River has provided sustenance, in so many ways, to the people of the region for tens of thousands of years. Since European settlement, it has been the bedrock of our agricultural and tourism sectors.

Throughout my life, I have seen the condition of the Murray deteriorate, and it continues to do so. I have also lived through drought. As is my nature, from time to time I have come up with ideas to help the region deal with both major problems.

From 2000 to 2010, we went through a decade of drought. It affected everyone. There's a limit to what one can do in such situations but one day, in late 2007, as I looked up and down the Deakin Avenue precinct and saw the historic native and imported trees and grass areas dead or dying, I decided that something needed to be done.

I rang up twenty people I did business with and asked each of them for a $1000 donation. In less than an hour they had pledged $20 000. Then I phoned the local water board, strongly suggesting, 'I want you to buy $20 000 worth of water and start bloody watering the lawn.' The place was revitalised in days, and we got a lot of attention. The most visual manifestation of the initiative was the switching on of the Chaffey fountain, that had been out of operation for several months due to water restrictions. I heard this put some noses out of joint in Swan Hill because they thought we were being given special treatment. They didn't realise we had paid for the water.

The following year, I proposed a scheme whereby the donation of water entitlements and cash to buy water could be used by local residents to water their lawns and gardens, which at the time was banned. Basically, my head just ran with ideas to stop the Sunraysia becoming a dustbowl. I am not a water vandal; I just think it is absurd to ask an entire community to see their green spaces dry out when in other sectors of the economy water is used with casual abandon.

In 2005, the Victorian Government was determined to establish a toxic waste dump at Hattah-Nowingi, near Mildura. The shock drove me into opposition mode. I did a lot of research and discovered that technology was available to destroy, rather than dump toxic waste, and that the process of destroying toxic waste was cheaper. So why would they even think about a dump? I debated the issue on radio with Victorian Industry Parliamentary Secretary, Carlo Carli; I alerted other media; and, helped get the community onside. My catch phrase became: 'Wouldn't it be better to destroy the toxic waste than destroy the Mallee?' Fortunately, the State government heard Mildura's complaints and ditched the project.

It hasn't just been Mildura that I've been interested in seeing reach its potential. In 2014, I proposed at least a partial solution, to the economic woes in the town of Wentworth, about 25 kilometres north-west of Mildura. I called for the headquarters of the Murray-Darling Basin Authority to be relocated from Canberra to Wentworth. The influx of 300 MDBA staff into the recently defunct Wentworth Services

Club building would have revitalised Wentworth no end. There was cheap housing in Wentworth and nearby towns, certainly much cheaper than Canberra; and Wentworth is on the Darling River, midway between the Hume Dam and the Lower Lakes in South Australia, about four hours by road from Adelaide, and less than two hours from the Menindee Lakes and Lake Victoria, all important storages in the Basin and vital to its functioning today. Unfortunately, the federal government gave short shrift to this idea.

Aspirations for a Tourist Town

Today, most people are not aware of the enormous significance of Mildura as a tourist destination from the 1950s to 1970s. That was the time before cheap flights to southeast Asia and the Pacific and globalisation. Honeymooners, families, campers, sporting clubs, businesspeople and others would flock to Mildura for a break from the Melbourne winters and cold weather everywhere.

Outside the realm of business, various tourism roles presented several opportunities to get into the life of the town. I participated as a creator and organiser, to financial backer and sponsor of events. Two events, in particular, helped to show what Mildura could do, so far as hosting and making welcome large numbers of visitors. They were an Australia-wide bowls tournament, and the Murray Valley Championship of Golf. The first took place over a month, and the second for about ten days. During the 1970s, these and many other events, as well as the good weather and the natural beauty of the area, helped expand our motel accommodation industry to service our tourists.

When many Australians think of tourism booms in the 70s, they think of the Gold Coast. After all, that place took off like mad from almost nothing. You may remember the main driving force of the Gold Coast boom was the businessman and mayor of the Gold Coast, Bruce Small.

When Bruce just had initial ideas for the Gold Coast, he wrote to our chairman of tourism in Mildura, a man named Dick Neville, and he asked Dick if he could come and attend one of our meetings, 'because you are the most successful tourist destination in Australia, and I want to know how you do it.' Of course, we proudly welcomed him to a meeting, and he asked many, many questions.

Next thing we hear that he's started up meter maids on the Gold Coast, a brilliant idea that attracted national media attention (though now we see it for its sexism and surprisingly it continues today). Next time I was up on the Gold Coast, I couldn't believe the difference from when I had been there a few years before. The place was booming, hotels everywhere.

Since the 1960s, I am proud to have done so much work to promote tourism and approach it from all angles, so many I cannot name them all. Even small things, such as having a five-metre long communal steel table constructed, and having a local artist create a ceramic depiction of Mildura on the table top, got me going. The table was erected outside Stefano's café. I was always looking for a way to express the town's creativity.

In 2005, I received an award recognising the 'Outstanding Contribution by an Individual' at the Powercorp PRIME

Sunraysia Daily, Wednesday June 1, 2011

Business Excellence Awards. While the award was for overall business excellence, a particular emphasis on the night was given to my contribution to tourism in the region. It's an award I value highly.

I took it upon myself to be a spokesperson on behalf of Mildura, and Sunraysia more generally, and that has been an ongoing commitment to this area as a tourist destination. For example, in 2006, I discussed plans with the then Liberal candidate for Mildura, Craig Bilstein, to have regional voices become more prominent in State government planning around tourism. The following year, I called for the establishment of an organisation that had responsibility for tourism along the Murray River, all the way from Albury to Goolwa. I keep dreaming.

In more recent years, I have become concerned that Mildura has lost its lustre and drive around bringing people from other places to come and visit. I have lobbied various groups, politicians and influential individuals to reignite the tourism flame, as it were, and once again to become a national leader in tourism, not a straggler, as it appears we are becoming.

La Famiglia

Like just about everyone, nothing is more important to me than family. And the person who was by my side for most of my adult and business life was, of course, my darling wife Anna.

Anna and I were very close in so many ways. We had the same sense and sort of vision; we had the same level of enthusiasm. Funnily, we were born within three days of each other, as Capricorns. Capricorns are said to be practical and ambitious—that's both of us.

Anna was a critical part of our success. I may have been the front man but behind the scenes, she was incredible. She was a fantastic hostess and presenter, very particular about what she did. I was a bit more casual than she was, but she made sure that I stuck to her rules. She taught me so much. Anna was meticulous, giving me an appreciation for how to dress properly and present everything with style—with all she did, she went out of her way to make sure things were spot-on.

One thing we loved doing together was travelling, though it took a while to start doing it. I basically worked from 1959 to 1975 without taking a proper holiday, though I always had that dream of visiting all the exotic places that I had heard and read about. My dream was always that, one day, when we could afford it, we were going to visit those places together. So, after going sixteen years without travel, we started doing exactly that.

In 1975, we took three months off and we did everything, without the kids. We wanted to have a sense of freedom, and you can't have that when travelling with kids, particularly ones so young. We left the girls with my mother and sister-in-law, Caterina.

We started off in Hawaii, then travelled down the west coast of America, to Acapulco, then New York, Boston, up to Canada, and across to Spain. Of course, we stayed a while in Italy, then picked up a car in Stuttgart and we continued travelling, through France and over to Monte Carlo and San Remo. It was such a memorable trip.

By the time we got back, Maria was calling my sister-in-law 'Mum'. Well, she was only three and her attitude to Anna was, understandably, like, 'Where have you been for the last three months?'

Apart from being a great travel companion, wonderful hostess, and brilliant mother, Anna supported my business activities. However, there were so many dramas over the years that, while her support never wavered, her desire to get involved certainly did. I can't blame her for that. She had seen people trying to pull us down so many times, that she stopped telling me 'go and do this or that'. Towards the end of her life, I made some business decisions without telling her, which I would never have done earlier. It's not that I was hiding things from her, I just didn't want her to worry.

While I had her support, there were many times when she urged me to slow down, or even stop for a while. In fact, she probably said that to me almost every day. The problem was, it's not in my nature to slow down, let alone stop.

Anna, on the other hand, was able to find that quiet spot. She found enormous solace in both the houses we built, particularly in their gardens. The second house we built was in Riverview Rise, Gol Gol. I bought the property in 1998, solely for Anna. She loved water and was a great swimmer, and the house backs right onto the Murray.

The property was part of a much larger one, some 200 acres of vineyards and citrus trees. Three developers subdivided it, so there were a number of lots for sale. Anna heard about it, went and had a look, and then urged me to go for a drive with her to see what I thought. She originally had her eye on a block two doors from the one we bought, as it was a little closer to the water, but I felt the block we eventually bought had better height. By the time of the auction, Anna did not have a preference, and, though she didn't come to the auction, she was delighted when I went home and told her one of the blocks was ours.

We designed the house together, started building it in 1999, and moved in on 25 March 2000. We had the garden designed by Paul Bangay, Australia's best-known European landscape gardener, and from the moment it was established, Anna put in so much work maintaining it and keeping it vibrant. My role was to mow the lawn—that was about it—whereas Anna put her entire energy into fruit trees, roses, a vegetable garden, a herbaceous garden, and the overall aesthetic of the place. She was passionate, and knew a lot. Not to mention, running the rest of the house, hosting family dinners, and all the duties that entailed.

In 2008, in the days just after Christmas, our lives were rocked when Anna discovered a lump in a breast, and was diagnosed with cancer. By then it was already stage four, and the general consensus of the specialists was that the breast

should be removed. However, because the tumour had already spread under an arm, it would be a major operation. We sought other advice and were basically left with two options: operate, as originally suggested, which would result in scars, possible infections or other complications, and not necessarily get rid of all of the cancer; or not operate and treat it with chemotherapy.

Our oncologist told us, 'I'll leave it to you to decide but if we leave it, Anna might not have long to go.'

We decided not to operate and to give Anna the best possible chemo treatment. We were told she may just live for six months but she lived another eleven years. I think one reason for that was that Anna was so meticulous with her medication. She was also so strong and positive, even when we had to change the chemotherapy, which we did several times because her body would become used to the chemo, which would then not be as effective.

We tried so many types of chemo, even a very expensive one we got from the United States, but none of them cured her. Despite the medication, all the other treatments, the dashed hopes and diminishing physical health, it's got to be said that over those eleven years, Anna made the most of life.

Then, suddenly, our oncologist had to deal with two cancer patients in the family. In 2015, I went to my dentist to have a sore tooth checked out. He gave me an injection to numb my gums and then touched something inside my mouth, that felt like someone stabbing me with a knife.

'I don't know,' he said. 'I've done 50 of these a day. I've done nothing different to what I normally do.'

When I got home, the pain continued and I went back to see the dentist. He took x-rays, found an infection and gave me tablets. The tablets didn't work and I eventually went to my doctor, who took a scan which turned out to show a tumour the size of an egg.

He told me it didn't look good, but I said, 'I respect you because you're my doctor, but I want a second opinion.' I rang a mate, Kevin Chambers, a top surgeon, then rang my daughter Donata, and we went to see him together.

The second opinion turned out to be as grave as the first, and preparations were made see a specialist. However, a combination of Easter holidays and the awkward position of the tumour meant the operation could not be done straight away. In the meantime, further samples were taken, and it was determined that my cancer was lymphoma, which is curable by chemotherapy.

That's the point at which Anna's oncologist suddenly had me as a patient as well. I had nine weeks of chemo, then a test that showed sixty per cent of the tumour had gone. I then had a further nine weeks of treatment, followed by more serious doses in hospital, which knocked me about so much I told him I wouldn't have any more of them. He insisted I continue with lower doses, which I did, and within weeks the tumour was gone. I had lost my hair, and 21 kilos, but beaten the cancer. My hair came back, along with some of the kilos, but so far, touch wood, not the cancer. I remember that time for one peculiar craving: the only thing I could tolerate was a daily bottle of our brewery's Sun Light beer!

During my treatment, Anna showed me again how wonderful a person she was. Despite her own battles, she sat beside me all the while I was in hospital.

After recovering, we decided to take a holiday overseas. It turned out to be our last one. We went to China in July 2017, and cruised along the Yangtze for ten days, took a train from Shanghai to Beijing and then home.

Unfortunately, things got worse for Anna the day after we returned. We were sitting at the breakfast table and she suddenly said, 'Oh, my legs are all jelly.'

I rang our family doctor, Don Hartely, who had been a constant presence in our lives. It was serious. I rang the oncologist and he told us to get straight down there. He did some tests and found another tumour, this one eating through her vertebrae. She was that close to becoming a quadriplegic. A surgeon operated the following morning and inserted a seven-inch pin into her vertebrae. All I could think of was, 'What if Anna had collapsed in China?' That would have been an absolute disaster and we certainly dodged a bullet.

Anna again showed her fighting spirit. The surgeon said she'd be walking within six weeks. She was walking in half that time, joking with her physiotherapist whom she nicknamed Mary Poppins.

Anna maintained her regime of chemotherapy until mid-2018 when she declared, 'I've had enough chemo, it's not going to improve me anymore.' On 10 August, we made our last trip to the oncologist, with Anna telling him, 'I don't want you to give me anymore medication, just give me pain killers so that I can control my pain.' That's exactly what she did, for the next four months.

While restrained in a chair, she was able to guide me and teach me many things such as cooking specific dishes and gardening skills and to clean up after myself. During the cooking lessons she would move into the kitchen in her wheelchair to teach me step by step what to do. Without too much fuss, she prepared me for a life without her. These were invaluable lessons and another example of the depth of her character.

Also in that time, Anna organised her own funeral with our daughters. She spent most of the day, in an armchair looking out onto her beloved garden and the Murray River. At some point, she wrote a note for me and slipped it between the cushion and the seat. The note said she was in peace and for me to look after the family. Anna died on 23 December 2018, and I found the note on Christmas Day.

That had already been a tough month, with my brother, Tony (Antonio), dying just twenty days before Anna in the Mildura Base ICU. My brother and I were like chalk and cheese. While I had an inner serious disposition, Tony was always jolly and appeared to be carefree. He raised a wonderful family of five children with his wife, Cathy, who also died suddenly. It was sad to see them go way before their time.

Tony, Anna, Cathy, Don

Tony had been a successful businessman in the region, primarily as a grape grower and property developer. He also gave back to the community through a number of local groups, including San Rocco, the Lions Club, Sunraysia Soccer Association and Three Colours Soccer Club.

Looking back on my family - specifically Anna, Donata, Maria and me - I don't think we could have been described as a typical Italian family. Apart from travelling on our own for so long that time, we were never really strict with the girls about what they could and couldn't do. We gave our girls a lot of freedom compared to many Italian post-war migrant families. We sent them away for a good education, and they have used both their education and their early skills in independent living to become successful in their own right.

We did, however, stress the importance of respect. I've always believed in behaving properly and about the way you speak. I hate people swearing. My father never swore in front of us. I insisted on good table manners; eating properly and not leaving the table while people were still eating, that sort of thing.

Daughters Maria Elizabeth and Donata

Despite having the same upbringing, Donata and Maria could not be more unlike. Donata is quiet and has that creative spirit. She was very close to Anna, and is like her in so many ways. Maria is, unusually for an Aries, more structured and formal; everything's got to be documented, spot on and done to the letter of the law. One thing they have in common, though, is that they are great mothers. They have brought up my grandchildren so well.

When the first grandchild, Domenico, was born, Donata and Stefano lived in the hotel. Domenico lived there for the first six years of his life in room 208. I often had my breakfast in the hotel dining room, and Domenico would sometimes join me in his pyjamas and dressing gown.

He's now a junior medical doctor, but even back then he had the attention for detail that doctors need. I once gave him a notebook and told him to go into every room in the hotel and find out how many light globes needed replacing. Well, he would come back with extensive reports about scratches on doors, markings on floors, and anything else that caught his attention.

One morning, Domenico got into the dining room before me, sat in my chair, and watched the waitresses in action. When the hostess passed him, Domenico got her attention, and said, 'My nonno wouldn't like to see you chitchatting like that. You should be working.' When she told me what had happened, I was very proud.

Domenico grew up to have a very gentle nature, just like Anna. I think that's why they were so close. Anna did everything for him. If he wanted the world, she'd go get it, right up to her dying moments.

Claudia, Donata and Stefano's daughter, has an enormous personality. She's the fun, charming, affectionate young woman who everybody loves. In short, she enjoys life to the full. She loves food, she loves wine, she loves travelling. I think she was only about six months when she was taken on her first trip, and she's hardly stopped travelling since.

Claudia was living overseas for most of Anna's last year, working in Amsterdam for a financial tech company, where she still works in corporate social responsibility. She returned home with her partner Mel five days before Anna died. Watching Claudia and her nonna together for those last days was joyous. Anna knew it was the last time she was going to see Claudia, and they had a fantastic time. Claudia modelled some of Anna's clothes, handbags, scarves and jewellery, and Anna was just grinning from ear to ear.

Claudia 2019

Domenico 2021

Maria's children still live close to me, and I make a point to visit them every day. Some grandparents might see their grandchildren occasionally. Again, I have been blessed by having the sort of relationships I do with my grandchildren. Maria and Mario have three boys, Massimo, Luca and Dante. Mario also has a son, Kurtis, from his first marriage. Anna and I treated Kurtis as another grandchild. There was nothing we would do with our grandsons without including him, and he regarded us as grandparents from the start. I cook for those boys regularly, and they love my pasta. I must say, I've learnt to make a good sauce: crushed tomato, garlic, onions, home grown basil, no meat.

I wouldn't want any of my grandchildren to go into business like I did. There are far better ways to make a living and have a good time than being stuck in a restaurant, serving people and then getting abused because it's too expensive or the food is not good enough. I have never encouraged my grandchildren to do what I did because I vividly remember the dramas that I had to go through. I had the passion, so could cope with the dramas, but they all appear to have different passions. Of course, Domenico and Claudia saw firsthand the sacrifices of that sort of life, through Donata and Stefano, and have taken very different career paths, thank goodness.

Kurtis, Anna, Mario, Don, Maria, Massimo, Dante and Luca

Anna was so proud of Domenico pursuing medicine. I love Claudia's entrepreneurial spirit; she'll be the chief executive of something one day and have a lot of fun in the meantime. Massimo is a true athlete and good academically. He loves football and wants to become the next Chris Judd. I reckon he may have a career there; he's passionate and he's a very good footballer. The other two are still too young to really know which direction they might take, and I'm not the type of grandparent who tries to push them this way or that. Luca and Dante are very affectionate towards me and I enjoy their company, especially taking them out for a meal or being in the passenger seat with Luca on his L's.

More Family

Charlie, Melissa, Georgia and Rohan Cann

Life doesn't stop surprising me. Just as you think your life has been as wonderful as anyone could wish for, something else springs up. For me, that was a phone call from a man claiming to be my son.

So let me take you back a few decades.

In the early 1960s, before I met Anna, I had a relationship with a nurse, Betty, who worked at Mildura Hospital. We were together for about twelve months, and then she fell pregnant with our baby. The news shocked me, as I certainly hadn't planned on having any children just yet. And back then, if you went to your parents and said, 'I've just met an Aussie girl, I've got her pregnant and I'm gonna marry her,' the shock to my parents would have been overwhelming. I loved my parents and I was concerned with how such a discussion would go and besides, I was not in a position to get married, I was only 22 and not ready for such a big commitment.

I told Betty I couldn't marry her, to which she responded very pragmatically, 'I don't care if you don't marry me but I'm still going to have our child. Even if adoption is the only option, I'm still going to have it.'

Betty remained in Mildura until she was about six months pregnant, then moved to Frankston in Melbourne to be with her sister. About two days before the birth of the child, she rang me and said, 'Listen Dom, if you want to come down to Melbourne, I'd like to say goodbye to you and spend the day with you.'

I jumped in the car and drove to Frankston. We had a wonderful day together. At the end of the day, we said our farewells and I drove back to Mildura. Two days later she rang and told me, 'I had a little boy and he's been adopted. I haven't seen him; I don't know what he looks like,' and that was the end of that. I lost contact with her completely.

About eight months after I married Anna, I told her, 'If a little boy comes a 'knocking on our door, don't be surprised. I've got a little boy running around the countryside.'

Anna, of course, took it all with good grace. We were blessed with two beautiful daughters, though in between Donata and Maria, Anna lost a son she was carrying. From that day on, Anna started asking me to look for this boy. She'd say, 'Why don't you look for him? Bring him in, I'll love him like I love the girls. It'll be no problem.' For years, whenever there was a story about a father/son reunion on TV, she would call me into the room and say, 'Look at this. After thirty-three years, a bloke just met his father, what about you? Go and look.'

'Where am I going to find him?' I'd say. 'My name isn't even on the birth certificate. I haven't got a clue where to start from.' This went on for fifty-three years, and remained a secret between Anna and me, or so I thought.

Shortly after Anna's death, Donata and I drove to Ballarat where Stefano's brother, Sergio, was giving an organ recital. On the trip back, Donata said to me, 'Dad, you've got a son, why didn't you tell me?'

I got a bit of a shock and I asked, 'Who the hell told you that?'

She said, 'Mum told me just before she died.'

'Forget about it, Donna,' I said, 'It's fifty-seven years gone, where are we going to find this bloke?'

That was the end of the conversation, and as far as I was concerned, the end of the matter.

Several weeks later, I received a letter in the mail at The Grand and the letter read:

> *Dear Mr Carrazza,*
>
> *My name is Rohan Cann. I would like to talk to you about a nurse who was in Mildura in the early 60s.*
>
> *If you want to get in touch, my phone number is ....*

I have to say, my immediate feeling was one of relief. I'd never acted on trying to find him, but after Anna talking about it for so long, it felt right.

I picked up the phone and introduced myself, then he said, 'Are you standing up or sitting down?'

'I'm standing up, but I know exactly what you're going to tell me.'

'What am I going to tell you?' he asked.

'That you're my son.'

'Yes, that's exactly what I'm going to tell you.'

Our contact would have occurred several years earlier, if not for a misunderstanding.

When Rohan turned forty, he tracked down Betty. Betty had married and had a family, and it turned out her son lived just two blocks away from Rohan, in Perth. They now see each other almost every day.

While Betty was happy to make contact, and to have a relationship with Rohan, for many years she refused to tell him who his father was. I now know that she had a friend from Mildura who kept her informed of what I was up to, who I had married, and how happy I was, and I believe she did not tell Rohan because she did not want to upset my life.

However, at some point, she gave Rohan a magazine that had me in it, and told him, "Your father's in there,' but she didn't tell him which one I was.

Rohan knew his father was from Mildura and had Italian background, so it did not take him too long to figure out that the person named Don Carrazza was most likely his father. He Googled my name and found an address. The problem was, my cousin is also Don Carrazza and he lives in Mildura, while I live just across the border. Of course, Rohan didn't know this, and sent a letter to my cousin.

My cousin's response was not surprising: 'Who is this madman writing me this letter. I wasn't even born then.' And he took no notice of it at all.

Rohan let it go for a couple of years and then tried again, this time with a registered letter. Whether it was the official nature of a registered letter, or because the writer was obviously persistent, Don rang the number on the letter, spoke to Rohan, and said, 'I don't know what you're talking about, I wasn't even born in 1961. I'm only 55 now.'

Rohan told Don he was looking for someone around eighty years old, and Don immediately told him about me, and said, 'If you send something to The Grand, he'll get it because he's got his office there.'

And that's where I got the letter.

After our first phone call, our intention was to catch up as soon as possible. He was in Perth and I was in Mildura but distance was not going to stop us. Something else did, though. The phone call took place in March 2020, and almost immediately, Australian states put up their borders due to Covid-19. For about eight months we corresponded by texts and talked on the phone.

There was also the matter of how to tell my family. I called a meeting of the whole family: Donna, Maria, Mario, Stefano, all my nephews and nieces, everyone, so there would be no surprises later. Of course, Donna knew about it, it wasn't a shock to her, but it was one hell of shock for Maria. because she didn't know about it—as it was for everyone else.

It was only when Donna told everyone that she had known about it for a short time and that Anna had told her, that everyone started to relax. They were worried that this had been a secret from Anna, but once that was cleared up, the mood changed to one of excitement, though still some shock. In hindsight, Anna did me a huge favour by telling Donna. If she hadn't, there would have been no third-party who could verify that Anna knew; some people may not have believed me, and who could have blamed them.

Our whole world changed. My daughters had a brother. Donna went from being the oldest child to the middle child, and I had two more beautiful granddaughters.

On 10 December 2020, at the first possible opportunity, I flew to Perth for the weekend to meet Rohan. I could have flown to Italy given the time it took. I left Mildura at 10am, flew to Melbourne, waited for a connection to Sydney, flew to Sydney, waited hours for another flight, and eventually got into Perth 15 hours after I had left home. It was late at night in Perth when I arrived, so I told them not to come to the airport; that we'd meet at my hotel the following morning.

The moment I saw Rohan, I knew he was my son. He's a big boy—takes after my grandfather; he had the same smile and eyes as other members of the family. Rohan had brought along his wife, Melissa. We then went to lunch where I also met their daughters, Charlotte and Georgia; and later, Melissa's parents. I felt welcome from the first moment I met them, and I welcomed them into my heart.

Strangely, my past collided with this new present life later that night.

Melissa's uncle had died a few days earlier, and he had been a passionate trotting man, even driving horses in races. To remember him, the family booked a room at the Gloucester Park harness racing meeting the night after I arrived, to which I was invited of course.

During the evening I met the manager of Gloucester Park and in passing, said to him, 'I haven't been here since 1982.'

'What did you come here for?' he asked.

'The Inter Dominion.'

'Did you have a horse?'

'Yes.'

'Which horse did you have?'

'Popular Alm.'

My Story: Living in Opportunity

And with that, he jumped up, exclaiming, 'Our CEO's got a picture of Popular Alm in his office', and ran off.

He returned, not with the picture, but with the CEO who wanted to meet me. And all of Melissa's family were wondering what I was doing with the CEO, because the CEO was quite some deal among them.

Over Easter 2021, Rohan and Melissa came to Mildura, and met the whole Carrazza clan. It was a very special occasion, of which many more will follow.

It's like a dream come true.

Extended family gathering Easter 2021

Far from Finished

I started as a businessman in the 1950s, and we're now into the 2020s. That's eight different decades in which I have conducted business. Many things have changed, but many remain the same. One thing's for sure, though. I am far from finished.

I still love property development, and for many years I had a vision for a residential and retail complex on a block just behind The Grand Hotel. The problem was it was the only block of land in the precinct that I didn't own. It was being used as a car park—a bright orange one at that—but the owners wouldn't sell it to me. It's not that they didn't want to sell. I believe they pursued other parties who weren't interested; they just didn't want to sell to *me*. Such was their stubbornness and jealousy that they preferred to make almost no money on the block than have me buy and develop the place. It may have been because they had been shareholders in The Grand when I bought it and they had lost their money and resented me, as did other investors who also lost their money.

This stand-off went on for several years. In the end, the owner got older, his kids saw the value in the property and sold it to me.

The block is about 1470 square metres, and will house twelve new units for the hotel, eight luxury residential units with views of the river, a shared garden and outdoor living space, a retail area, and 32 car spaces. When it's up, there won't be a better place to live (or stay) right in town.

City Garden Apartments on Deakin Avenue

I have another development I would love to see materialised, a vision not unlike the one I had for the casino, convention and entertainment complex. It's for a conference centre, hotel and marina, and I want to develop it in memory of my father and brother. I'm doing it with my nephew Joseph, Antonio's son. We've been at it for years, producing design after design, report after report, speaking to this person and that person.

One day, fingers crossed.

I know I don't have to keep working but I love the feeling of being involved, and progress. And I'm doing it now, not for myself but for the future of our region, the future of my grandchildren, and for the future of the whole community. And, for the fun of it. I know how important business opportunities are to the region. After all, over the years thousands of people have been employed through our restaurants, hotel, brewery, and all those other (ad)ventures, and though having a job is not everything, it is something.

It hasn't been easy, as I have had to fight for all that I've achieved and that Mildura has gained. Certainly, though, it's been worth it.

Tributes

Dante Mammone

My nonno is naughty. He brought me goldfish and a kitten without asking Mum because he knew I wanted more pets. He is always on time when he picks me up for any occasion. I am lucky as I never knew my other grandfather. Nonno is a big part of our lives. He visits us every night without fail.

Luca Mammone

Nonno is one of the strongest and most intelligent people in my life.

Nonno came over from Italy on a boat when he was very young. How incredibly brave of him to do something like that! Me, I would have never had the guts to travel on a boat, leaving everything behind that I knew and loved, for this new place that I would barely know.

I will always have the memories of my brothers and I going out for dinner and lunch with Nonno. Of him telling us his stories and me thinking how proud his parents must have been about him accomplishing so much when he was young and still, to this day.

Nonno, also at lunch and dinner, loves talking about the garden that he and Nonna created together. I always think of the garden as an escape for Nonno, as it would be one of the times that he wouldn't think about business or other things on his mind. It is a bit like Narnia, because when you are there you just appreciate pure nature and forget about everything else.

Quite recently I have got my L's. Nonno and I love going for drives. On one such drive Nonno showed me all the businesses he has owned in his lifetime in Mildura and that was quite impressive.

Nonno has supported and helped our family a lot, never not spoiling us. I love you Nonno.

Massimo Mammone

Relentless, powerful and generous. Always gentle however robust, tough love.

Nonno, our dinners out on a Friday or Saturday night are memories that will live with me forever. Your stories and experiences never failed to entertain and usually had the boys and I in awe or laughing uncontrollably. Our bonding through football and love for our hopeless Carlton has always given us something to talk about.

Your passion for anything that you do is unmatched by anyone, your ability to have a vision then take action and turn your dream into reality is truly incredible. It is a quality that I am developing in order to carry on your hard-working legacy.

You have always been present in my life and always made an effort to support me in anything that I do: at my football matches, school events and any special occasion. I am grateful for your involvement and guidance.

All families have problems and issues, and sometimes your will and desire to create your vision has caused turbulence within the household. However, you have always put your family first and showed unconditional love no matter the circumstance.

The loss of Nonna was full of heartbreak and grief. Despite her death, her spirit lives on through us, and your connection with her through the garden is very special and sacred. Without Nonna's support, love and at times tolerance, your journey may not have been as exciting or successful. She was a strong independent woman who helped shape you into the man you are today. I will always remember her words of keeping things 'simple but elegant'.

Our Italian culture and history is something that I am proud of and hold close to my heart. You brought this culture to the Sunraysia area and created an atmosphere and environment that had never been seen before. You were a pioneer.

I have learnt so much from you and I am proud and grateful to call you my Nonno and to have you in my life. Your lessons of hard work and discipline will be embedded in my mind for the rest of my life. Your constant desire to learn and be educated regardless of age is something I will also carry with me. And your ability to reach your goals and turn your dreams into reality, is a skill I intend to implement and perform in my life.

Nonno, I love you, thank you for everything. Can't wait to see you soon.

Family man, businessman and man of the people, my nonno.

Charlie Cann

I always knew my dad was adopted. I was young when dad found Betty, so I don't clearly remember meeting her. Dad imagined meeting his birth father, and for years he tried to make contact. I remember one specific conversation. We were on a walk, and it was a topic that always came up. Dad was running scenarios in his head about the reasons as to why his birth father hadn't responded. I just said to him, what have you got to lose. Try one more time.

It was a Friday. I was on my way to work when dad called, saying he spoke to his birth father. I could hear in his voice how beyond happy he was, and I started crying with happiness. A weight had just been lifted, and my dad felt complete.

Charlie and Georgia Cann

Dad and Nonno began calling regularly, and dad would relay the conversation to us. We just wanted to meet him, but Covid and our Mum's fear of flying made it difficult. Eventually, we were all able to get together when Nonno came to Perth. The first time we saw Nonno, we could see the kindness and joy in his face, like we see in our dad's, and although we had never met, he seemed familiar.

Since our first meeting, unfortunately, we aren't able to spend as much time together as we would like, but luckily Nonno loves a chat and is quick on the text. However, phone records show that Georgia is a bit slow on the communication but hopes to improve.

Claudia de Pieri

My memories growing up in the hotel are some of the fondest I have from childhood. In those memories you are there, directing the staff and the hotel operations as if we were on a Hollywood movie-set. I remember our breakfasts in the Chandelier Room, where we would sit at the same table every morning, eating triangle toasts with butter and honey, me drawing or talking your ear off while you kept one eye on the staff at work. I remember you walking around the hotel with your ironed shirts and a comb in your front chest pocket. Even though you didn't like it, I would sometimes quickly ruffle your stiff hair for a giggle, and just as quickly you would whip out that comb and slick everything back in its place, side-glancing at me with a look which said you weren't happy but you weren't going to reprimand me either.

Growing up, I was the only granddaughter in a sea of grandsons. And while most traditional patriarchs would focus their attention on the first-born son, you looked out for me and made me feel extra special.

You are my greatest cheerleader. Thank you for your constant encouragement and when it's needed, your reinforcing support. You're always there for me, whether it's along my path in business, or helping to design and renovate my Amsterdam apartment. Even 17 000km of distance won't stop your involvement in a building project!

For the record, we both have a lot in common: we both love to explore new territory, our entrepreneurial spirits get excited by the prospect of the new, or of a challenge, and we both love to tell stories (with a flair of over-exaggeration and self-promotion).

Being unable to travel to visit you in Australia due to COVID-19 has been challenging, however our weekly Sunday calls are something I treasure. We keep them short and sweet but full of meaning, saying everything we both need to say. The connection we share is strong, and I often feel like you are carrying me around near your heart, like you did when I was little.

Tuo tesoro di nonno, Claudia

Domenico de Pieri

If one can, imagine a plough in a field of dense Buronga floodplain clay, being pulled by a decades-old, sun-baked tractor, one that has never broken down and one that its owner might call "trusty and reliable" with masked affection: well, that combination—a source of energy, and an inexorably driven thing—might sum Nonno up. Nonno is all about gut-instinct and trusting it as far as it will take him. He could be described as gung-ho—that story of him turning up to his first day of work without even knowing what the job was is a case in point—but this is a reflection of his enthusiasm for work, for getting things done, for what he calls, 'Progress' with all the conviction of a priest. What is noteworthy, though, is that he is more than a model of a machine. He embraces his grandchildren with all the warmth and security of a benevolent *paterfamilias*; and, as I have grown up, I have become aware of his awareness of how life truly is fleeting, of how there is not time to discuss and to dawdle and deliberate. He is a man of action and through that a man of love, and he will deal with the consequences later, no matter what they may be, with a quiet calm and confidence. Of course, he knows his limits too, embodied through his horse-betting habits, very healthy attitude to food and drink (except ice-cream), and his general business acumen that has developed over decades. If there were ever a human definition of conviction and magnanimity, it would be Domenico Carrazza, known to me as Nonno.

Kurtis Mammone

While you are known to others as The Don, Mr C or Mr Carrazza, I have been privileged to call you Nonno. I have felt part of your family from a young age, even though we are not blood relatives. I was somewhat nervous around you and intimidated by you when I was home on school holidays as a kid. After all, you cut a powerful figure and still do. I knew I never wanted to be in your bad books. I am still not sure you will ever forgive me for forgetting to make your coffee three days in a row at the café!

Nonno, you're not just The Don, but an influential figure, an inspiration, family man, entrepreneur, someone I have admired and looked up to ever since I can remember. Being able to watch and learn through your ventures and accomplishments and the legacy you've created and continue to create has been an honour. What I have gained from watching and listening to your life stories — from the hotel to the racehorses — are memories I will cherish. I am thankful for everything I have learnt from you. I'll continue to learn as much as I can and keep creating memories. I am happy to have given you a new title to carry as a Great Nonno.

Mario Mammone

I have known Don since 1989. He was my first boss until I married Maria in 1999 when he became my father-in-law. I was at the Grand Hotel when he took over. My admiration for who were to become my future in-laws developed before I even met Maria. He has always given me advice and guidance in all my businesses. Without doubt, he is never shy to tell me if what I am doing is not up to his standards. I am grateful for the deep love he has for my four sons. I respect and admire his strong work ethic and he never ceases to amaze me with his determination to get a job done.

Maria Carrazza

The perfect father-daughter relationship that I have wished for is far from the bond I share with my father. Our duo is complicated; many say we are alike, which is why we butt heads often. He has always called out injustice, told me to question everything and to fight for what I believe in. For him, you treat people equally: the hotel cleaner is just as important as the hotel manager. His love for my four boys brings such a fullness to my heart. For that I am grateful and love him more than he could imagine.

Stefano de Pieri

Domenico Carrazza, affectionately known as Dad or Nonno to his family, or Mr C to his employees, is a complex man who is often misunderstood, especially by those who are unable to penetrate his reserve. And there lies one of his contradictions: a man who has devoted his life to hospitality and demonstrates warmth to his guests and generally comes alive in company, can be simultaneously taciturn and reserved. It took me a while to figure that out and perhaps the answer to many questions about the Don's personality will be found in this story.

A well-known politician once told me why he thought that the Don was attracting criticism and jealousy. DC, he said, has excelled on all fronts, he has covered all the fields of endeavour and no one could easily pigeon hole and relegate him to this variant or other of the classic successful migrant and be put in his place. He has been a company director, a publican, a restauranteur, a very good farmer – albeit on a small scale – a government man, a successful horse owner (read gambler), a creative force, a football committee man and more. In a culture where tall poppies are mowed down, he has made himself an obvious target. In all those facets of work he has been as good if not better as any of his critics.

At the time of writing this I have worked for him, with him or near him in one form or another for thirty years. We have had furious, angry arguments, we have entertained crazy ideas, fabulous projects, celebrated success and commiserated failures, such as could have destroyed less resilient people. One of his virtues is the capacity to see things as they should or could be rather than how they are. I think this is the migrant's eye combined with a natural enthusiasm to improve things. Another, certainly not an obvious one, a tolerance of people and their shortcomings, including the capacity to forgive. I have learnt a lot from him and for that I am grateful.

On our first meeting he accused me of eating too slowly, and that was to him a sign of people who are not fast enough at their work!

That was not a promising start, but over time I have gained enormous respect for this man who, in many ways, has been like a second father to me.

Donata Carrazza
Two impressions and an image of my father

The Game

The room is rectangular, the kitchen table has six figures seated around it. The one woman in the room, her mother, is preparing food.

"Here's my girl. Can't sleep?"

She runs to her father, his large hands lifting her onto his lap. The cigar he is sucking on is put to rest in an ashtray that is full of ash and cigarette butts. The residual smoke hangs above all of them like a cloud.

The table is covered with a thick, chequered blanket. Another three ashtrays dot the surface like landmines. Bill notes are piled in the middle, some of them folded and worn, others new and pristine.

With her arrival, the men have lain their own hand of cards face down on the table. Any tension she noticed on their faces has lifted. They look at her benignly, some of them even smile.

The child allows her little body to mould into the animal warmth of her father's frame, one side of her face rooting into his chest.

"Ok fellas, let's have a break."

Maurice tickles her foot while downing a mouthful of scotch. He has a gorilla playfulness she finds funny. She giggles and arches her back. The other men have broken into conversation about why they don't mind losing at these games since Anna's food makes up for it.

She likes these men and their ritual gathering. It is different to the other things that take place in the kitchen. It is like a secret that they are not supposed to talk about to anyone else.

What if she were allowed to stay and watch? She could observe from her father's knee and he might even instruct her quietly, whispering information into her ear, until the numbers, shapes and images on those cards started to make sense. Then he might get her to notice the way each man uses his face and body to distract or obscure.

The next lesson might be about how to project confidence. In other words, how to bluff. To tap the table with arrogant indifference for another card, to draw from your half Corona, timing it so that the smoke you exhale snakes languidly above you. (Smokers who jab their cigarette like a dart in and out of their mouths are dead give-aways). To keep your attention on the others without ever forgetting every action you make, every word you say. These are the lessons she might learn.

Instead, she gets to drink a warm cup of Milo and watches her mother adorn the table, now cleared of money and cards, with platters of Welsh rarebit oozing melted cheese and smelling of mustard. The quiet ones like Tony and her father become animated and vocal about the deliciousness of the snack.

The interlude in the kitchen is over too soon. It is time for her to go back to bed. Before her mother sweeps her tired little body into her own, she kisses her father goodnight and smiles farewell to the men.

A story my father told me

He whistled by placing his thumb and middle finger inside his mouth against his rolled tongue. His signal was returned just as loudly from the dock where thousands of people were gathered, waving and crying. Every set of eyes were fixed on the *Neptune* as it churned water at its stern, the rudder guiding the bow away from the Bay of Naples. From the ship he couldn't identify his young uncle among the uplifted arms and the swaying bodies–they all seemed to breathe as one entity. It didn't matter. He could hear him. They both whistled back and forth, gaining the attention of those closest to them, who gave each of the boys more space and watched their farewell game with benign forbearance.

This photo was part of an exhibition at Gallery 25 called Portrayed. It featured Mildura identities in highly contrived poses. I wanted to poke fun at my Dad's infamy as a mafioso drug dealer. My greatest regret was not lighting that cigar!
Photo credit: Kristian Haggblom

Rohan Cann

On the sixth of March 2020, some 56 years after my birth, a seven-minute phone call changed my life. It was at this moment I met my biological father for the first time, be it only by phone. In those first moments, Don's voice projected an instant sense of friendship, excitement, and a desire to connect. This is the man I am proud to be able to call my biological father.

From that day on, we maintained contact. Of course, Covid managed to get in the way, but as soon as there was an opportunity, Don made the journey West, although it was a bit of an unorthodox route, and, as he says, he could have flown to Europe in the time it took.

Ten months had passed. We had spoken weekly, sent texts, and exchanged pictures. As an adopted child, there were times that I had questions that couldn't be answered. What were my bio parents like? Did I have any siblings? Did my birth father care about my birth mother, or was it a one-night stand? Were they nice people? Did they have good health? So many questions. But at the end of the day, I think I just wanted them to care.

I was very fortunate to be able to find my biological mother just prior to my 40th birthday. She and her family welcomed my family and me with open arms. So, as my wife Melissa and I left the hotel elevator in search of Don's room, all these flashbacks and thoughts were running through my mind. Melissa, my human shield, was in front as always, there to support me. Don appeared from the shadows of his room's doorway, and although we had been speaking for months, I still felt apprehensive and did not know what to expect. Was it going to be a handshake, a light embrace, or just 'hi son'? This smartly dressed man, with a beaming smile, stepped forward and hugged Melissa. I instantly felt calm, a sense of familiarity. Then we embraced for the first time, and for me, at that moment, I felt a feeling of true happiness.

I couldn't have asked for a better version of a 'Bio Dad'. Don is a charismatic man, educated, worldly, a great communicator, has a good sense of humour with a wonderful love of family.

We had three perfect days together. We were able to get a real understanding of each other, and he got to meet my family, extended family, and friends. Don is a great storyteller. He told me stories of his life's adventures, trips abroad, business ventures, and the very funny love story of how he met his wife, Anna.

If there is a downside to this story, it would be the fact that I was unable to meet two very special people in my father's life. Anna and his brother Antonio 'Tony' Carrazza. Unfortunately, they had both passed just a couple of years before us making contact. I am unsure why, but with Anna especially, I feel some close bond, and I think we would have been good friends. Happily, for me, both Anna and Tony live on through their children, who I have since been able to meet. Donata and Maria, my two beautiful sisters radiate their mother's presence and Tony's children made my family and I feel very welcome when we visited the following Easter.

On Sunday, the last day of Don's stay, he asked me if we could take a drive to the north of Perth as he had someone he wanted to visit. It turned out that Don had an employee from Mildura who was in Perth visiting his ill brother. This simple act of kindness, the fact that with all that was going on in his own life, Don wanted to make time to visit this man and his dying brother, showed me the measure of the man. I can proudly call Dominic (Don) Carrazza my Biological Father.

Our first meeting as a complete family

Acknowledgements

80th birthday celebrations

At almost 82 years of age, it has been a rewarding exercise to work on this book project and to try and capture my life in its pages. I hope it contributes to yet another understanding of the post-war migrant experience. My sincere thanks to Nic Brasch for shaping my words into my life story. I have been fortunate to have dear friends around me: they know who they are and I want to thank them for their love and support over the years. Likewise, I would like to acknowledge the loyal employees who have assisted me in the course of my business life. Lastly, deep gratitude to my family for their ongoing love and support.

80th birthday celebrations

www.ingramcontent.com/pod-product-compliance
Lightning Source LLC
Chambersburg PA
CBHW061231070526
44584CB00030B/4070